Classic Pens

CLASSIC SPORTS
Jonathan Knight, Series Editor

Classic Bucs: The 50 Greatest Games in Pittsburgh Pirates History
    David Finoli

Classic Steelers: The 50 Greatest Games in Pittsburgh Steelers History
    David Finoli

Classic Browns: The 50 Greatest Games in Cleveland Browns History
Second Edition, Revised and Updated
    Jonathan Knight

Classic Cavs: The 50 Greatest Games in Cleveland Cavaliers History
Second Edition, Revised and Updated
    Jonathan Knight

Classic Pens: The 50 Greatest Games in Pittsburgh Penguins History
Second Edition, Revised and Updated
    David Finoli

Classic Pens

THE 50 GREATEST GAMES IN PITTSBURGH PENGUINS HISTORY
Second Edition, Revised and Updated

David Finoli

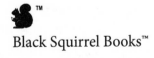

Black Squirrel Books™

Kent, Ohio

To my father Domenic: Thank you for the joy of sport and life that you have instilled in me: you are truly missed.

Black Squirrel Books™
Frisky, industrious black squirrels are a familiar sight on the Kent State University campus and the inspiration for Black Squirrel Books™, a trade imprint of The Kent State University Press. www.KentStateUniversityPress.com.

ISBN 978-1-60635-307-3
Manufactured in the United States of America

Cataloging information for this title is available at the Library of Congress.
21 20 19 18 17   5 4 3 2 1

Contents

Acknowledgments

I've had a fine career writing about the wonderful teams that Western Pennsylvania has produced, but the excitement and joy that the 2015–16 Pittsburgh Penguins gave the great fans of the Steel City on their way to the franchise's fourth Stanley Cup was truly a site to behold, the memories of which are a perfect addition to my book *Classic Pens*.

Projects such as this are never complete without the incredible support of many, most importantly my wonderful family that includes my wife, Vivian, as well as my children, Matthew, Tony, and Cara.

My extended family has always been a source of support over the years, no matter where I've been and what I've accomplished. My brother, Jamie; his wife, Cindy; my nieces, Brianna and Marissa; my sister, Mary; her husband, Matthew; my aunts, Maryanne and Betty; my cousins, Fran, Luci, Flo, Beth, Tom, Gary, Linda, Amy, Amanda, Claudia, Ginny Lynn, Pam, Debbie, Diane, Vince, and Richard; as well as the memories of my mother, Eleanor; my father, Domenic; my cousins, Tom Aikens and Eddie DiLello; my Uncle Vince; my grandparents; and my aunts Louise, Norma, Jeannie, Libby, Mary, and Evie have all been essential in any success I've enjoyed in my life. A thank-you also has to go to my in-laws, Vivian and Salvatore Pansino, for their continual support.

At my alma mater, Duquesne University, I had the pleasure of witnessing my first Penguin games in person and developed a love of Penguin hockey that continues to this day. Luckily, I had a great core of friends who accompanied me to those memorable contests. I continue to discuss the team's exploits to this day with such distinguished alumni as Chris Fletcher, Bill Ranier, Dan Russell, Gary Kinn, Rich Boyer, Matt O'Brotka, Shawn Christen, Gary Degnan, and Bob O'Brien.

Finally, a thank-you goes to the great people of The Kent State University Press, such as Will Underwood, Mary Young, and Classic Sports editor Jonathan Knight, who have been wonderful partners on four of my books in the past as well as this one.

Introduction

Sitting in my seat at the Consol Center before Game Two of the Stanley Cup finals next to my good friend Rich Boyer, I just kept thinking what a surreal feeling it had been seeing this club get to this point. Only a few months before it appeared that the window for winning a Stanley Cup had been closed shut. It was only nine short years ago in 2007 when a young team led by Sidney Crosby, Evgeni Malkin, and Marc-Andre Fleury turned the Penguins from losers into contenders. Two years later they captured the franchise's third Stanley Cup, as the word dynasty was constantly mentioned as the ultimate potential for this squad.

With a window for more championships wide open, injuries began to mount, especially to their core of stars, and playoff disappointments became commonplace. As late in 2015 approached, Crosby looked as if his career was coming to a screeching halt, coach Mike Johnston had lost control of the team, and they were out of a playoff spot.

Discussions went from titles to serious thoughts that the team should rebuild ASAP. It had been this way so many times in the history of the Pittsburgh Penguins, especially before the emergence of Mario Lemieux. Just as the window was being locked shut, Penguins general manager Jim Rutherford made a couple astute deals adding Carl Hagelin and Trevor Daley in exchange for the slower David Perron and Rob Scuderi. He also looked toward his AHL affiliate and brought up the likes of Conor Sheary, Bryan Rust, and Tom Kuhnhackl. Add to the mix other former Wilkes-Barre Penguins in goaltender Matt Murray, who took over for an injured Fleury, and the Baby Penguins coach Mike Sullivan, who replaced the Johnston, and remarkably the rebuilding of the Pens took literally weeks rather than years—perhaps the quickest rebuilding job in the history of professional sports.

This team surprisingly went from the biggest disappointment in the Steel City to the darlings of this wonderful city. They played many exciting contests on their way to the Stanley Cup championship that deservingly sit next to the best games this franchise had played from days gone by; the Lemieux era, the first Stanley Cup runs, and the days when the team wore blue as their primary colors.

As Game Two came to a dramatic end with Sheary scoring a magnificent overtime goal, Rich, myself, and over 18,000 of the Penguin nation erupted in the Consol Center, louder than anytime I had ever heard it. They had just witnessed what is now one of the 50 greatest games the Penguins have ever played. As the franchise enters its fiftieth season, that game, along with a few more from this remarkable campaign, are proudly added to the second edition of *Classic Pens*. May many more great moments and games follow.

#50

Yes, We Belong

It was only a few months before that the local and national media were lamenting about the fall of what used to be the perennial Stanley Cup champion contending Pittsburgh Penguins.

It was hard to believe that it was so recent that this team was talked about as one of the best in its era. With two of the all-time greats at their disposal in Sid Crosby and Evgeni Malkin, it seemed like this club always had an opportunity to add a fourth Stanley Cup to the franchise's illustrious arsenal; remarkably as the 2015–16 season was unfolding, both Malkin and Crosby looked old, way past their prime.

Since the middle of the prior campaign, the team had forgotten how to score. The Pens were now considered one of the worst, if not the worst, offensive squads in the National Hockey League. With a farm system that seemingly had no prospects capable of adding potential help to this struggling franchise, there was very serious doubt that they even belonged in the Stanley Cup playoffs, a spot that seemed like their yearly birthright.

When the team's front office decided to fire first general manager Ray Shero and then their coach Dan Bylsma, they surprisingly brought in former Carolina GM Jim Rutherford, who had many critics for the job he had done late in his tenure with the Hurricanes, to lead the Pens fortunes. After he had seemingly failed to bring in a big name to coach the team, he settled on a junior hockey coach by the name of Mike Johnston. It was a heavily criticized move that became even more so when the coach was unable to coax what appeared to be a highly skilled offensive juggernaut to actually put the puck in the net.

The Pens actually got off to a quick start early in the 2014–15 campaign but quickly became mediocre due to their offensive futility. After a quick exit from

1

the playoffs and a 15–10–3 start the following year, which saw them muddle in fifth place while falling to 28th in the league in scoring, Rutherford decided it was time to own up to his mistake by letting go of Johnston, claiming that "we're not far from the top of the division, but we're not far from the bottom either. It's never a comfortable time. It's bothered me, but I felt it was necessary."[1]

Pittsburgh Post-Gazette writer Paul Zeise went one better after the team won the Eastern Conference title saying that "we could talk all day about the other moves (Phil Kessel, Eric Fehr, Nick Bonino, etc.) Rutherford made, but I'd argue none of them would be relevant if he didn't first correct the mistake he made by firing Johnston."[2]

He hired former Bruins coach Mike Sullivan, who was the current Wilkes-Barre Penguins head man, to replace Johnston; while the results would eventually be spectacular, they weren't at first. They won only six of the first 16 games under their new coach, and even though they played better, they were still mediocre entering March. Add to the situation that Malkin had seriously injured his elbow and one could see that things were not looking good for hockey in the Steel City. A funny thing happened when things appeared to be at their worst for this team; the players finally started to react to their new coach as he adjusted the game plan to take advantage of their talents. As for their oft-criticized GM, he was quietly adding speed, trading for the fast Carl Hagelin and Trevor Daley, as well as finally realizing that he had talent in Wilkes-Barre, adding Bryan Rust, Conor Sheary, and Scott Wilson to the roster.

The team was now younger and faster, winning the first three games after Malkin went down and four in a row overall. While getting better, they still were not considered a dangerous threat to do anything in the Stanley Cup playoffs; in fact, there was still a possibility they would miss out for the first time in nine years. They were going to Philadelphia to face the hottest team in the league, a team that had run off an 8–1–1 streak to put themselves squarely back in the playoff hunt. Led by Claude Giroux and Wayne Simmonds, they were breathing down the Penguins neck and looking to use this contest to show their new power was not a fleeting thing; Pittsburgh was hoping to do the same. In the end, the now offensively potent Penguins showed the NHL it needed to take them seriously—not just with their scoring talents but also because of their suffocating defense.

It didn't look good early on when the Flyers Radko Gudas scored quickly in the second period, burying the puck behind Marc-Andre Fleury to give Philadelphia a 1–0 lead with 1:58 gone in the period. After a year and a half of troubled moments, this felt like it could have been the straw that might have sent the team back into their malaise; instead, it became the beginning of its championship run.

A minute later Nick Bonino, he of the legendary Punjabi Hockey Night in Canada radio call, fought for the puck with the Flyers Shayne Gostisbehere and found Daley. Daley beat Philadelphia goalie Steve Mason, who was starting for the ill Michal Neuvirth, to tie the contest at one.

While the game was even on the scoreboard, the goal by Daley invigorated the Penguins, who began to dominate their cross-state rivals. They showed Philadelphia—and the other teams in the NHL—that they not only could score, but they could also cut off the other team's offense. In a strategy that eventually became their calling card on their way to the Stanley Cup title, they held their opponents to very few shots, making life easy for the goalies that wore the Penguins logo on their chest.

After giving up only four in the first, they outshot the Flyers significantly in the second period but were unable to take advantage until late in the frame when the much maligned Phil Kessel stole the puck from Ryan White before passing it to Bonino who found an open Hagelin, putting the Pens ahead 2–1. It foreshadowed things to come as the newly formed HBK line (Hagelin, Bonino, Kessel) was now a force. Just 89 seconds later, a Chris Kunitz slap shot went wide but bounced off the boards against the back of Mason into the net for a two-goal advantage at the end of two.

Outshooting the hot Flyers 27–9 going into the third, Pittsburgh kept their intense defensive pressure up, allowing only eight in the final period to hold on for the victory. Kris Letang scored a controversial empty net goal late in the contest, appearing to kick in the puck, which caused it to initially be overturned before the powers that be recanted and allowed the final score. It was inconsequential though; the Pittsburgh Penguins had dominated their rivals, which began an incredible streak that would culminate with the franchise's fourth Stanley Cup. It was the defining moment in the regular season where the Pens showed they were truly contenders; they showed they really belonged.

BOXSCORE

Team	1	2	3	F
Pittsburgh	0	3	1	4
Philadelphia	0	1	0	1

Per	Team	Goal (Assist)	Time
2	Philadelphia	Gudas 4	1:58
2	Pittsburgh	Daley 5 (Bonino, Fehr)	2:59
2	Pittsburgh	Hagelin 9 (Bonino)	16:56
2	Pittsburgh	Kunitz 15 (Crosby, Hornqvist)	18:25
3	Pittsburgh	Letang 14 (Kunitz, Crosby) EN	18:22

Team	Goalie	Saves	Goals
Pittsburgh	Fleury	16	1
Philadelphia	Mason	31	3

Shots	1	2	3	T
Pittsburgh	11	16	8	35
Philadelphia	4	5	8	17

PENGUINS 6, MINNESOTA NORTH STARS 4
MAY 23, 1991

The Glorious Steam Bath

One only needs to look at the picturesque setting of the NHL's annual Winter Classic, played outdoors every New Year's Day, to see that hockey is truly a cold-weather game, but Game Five of the 1991 Stanley Cup Finals was anything but a cold-weather contest. With Pittsburgh in the middle of a late-May heat wave, the outdoor conditions resembled a tropical atmosphere. While Civic Arena was equipped to maintain an ice rink, as one of the oldest buildings in the league, it didn't have centralized air conditioning. The arena resembled more of a steam bath than a hockey rink when 16,164 overheated fans watched as the hometown Penguins and Minnesota North Stars took the ice to break their two-games-apiece series deadlock.

While this was the first time the Penguins had ever played in the finals, they were still the prohibitive favorites. Champions of the Patrick Division, Pittsburgh faced a Minnesota team that snuck into the playoffs with a mere 68 points. Minnesota, the last seed in the Norris Division, upset the conference's top two seeds before defeating the Edmonton Oilers in five games to capture the Campbell Conference crown and a place in the Stanley Cup Finals.

The upstart North Stars then took two of the first three games from the Penguins and were looking to take a stranglehold on the series before Pittsburgh halted their momentum with a 5–3 victory in Game Four. Now the teams traveled back to the Steel City for a critical—and steamy—Game Five.

The Penguins, who were held in check for the first three games by goalie John Casey, seemed to have solved his dominance in Game Four, and the trend continued into the fifth game, as they knocked Casey out of the game with four goals in the first 14 minutes.

Mario Lemieux started the early onslaught when he beat Casey with a power-play goal at the 5:36 mark before his line mate, Kevin Stevens, added a power-play goal of his own five minutes later to stretch the advantage to two. Pittsburgh right winger Mark Recchi, who'd picked up the scoring slack for the Pens during the regular season when Lemieux missed 50 games to injury, then came to life after a quiet series to score twice within two minutes to give Pittsburgh a 4–0 lead with 6:19 remaining and send Casey to the bench. "We came out skating," Recchi said. "And when we do that, we're a very effective team."[1]

Minnesota would not go quietly. As effective as the Penguins' power play had been at the beginning of the game, it would be just the opposite as the first period was coming to an end when Minnesota's Neil Broten knocked in a shorthanded tally to cut the lead to three. Then the tide started to turn against Pittsburgh. Starting goalie Tom Barrasso was pulled from the game after suffering a minor groin pull, and backup Frank Pietrangelo entered the contest. Minnesota welcomed Pietrangelo by scoring a second shorthanded goal seven minutes into the second period, stunning both the home crowd and the Penguins themselves. "It seems like they're putting their scorers to kill penalties and we've got to be aware of that," Pittsburgh right wing Joe Mullen said. "We've got to make sure we get back and help the defensemen."[2]

With the game, and potentially the Stanley Cup, seemingly slipping away, Pittsburgh center Ron Francis—destined for hockey's Hall of Fame—picked up his team by slipping a shot past Minnesota backup goalie Brian Hayward to restore Pittsburgh's three-goal lead as the second period came to an end.

With the steamy arena at a fever pitch as the final period began, the North Stars refused to surrender. At the 1:36 mark, Ulf Dahlen buried one past Pietrangelo to cut the advantage to 5–3; then six minutes later the enthusiastic crowd was further quieted as Minnesota's David Gagner netted the twelfth goal of his impressive playoff run to pull the North Stars within a goal with less than 13 minutes to play.

Minnesota continued to put pressure on Pietrangelo, but the Penguins' backup preserved the lead with several amazing saves as the clock was winding down. With less than two minutes left and the score still 5–4, Pittsburgh defensive left wing Troy Loney came aggressively in on the Minnesota goal. Broten shoved Loney into the crease as Penguin defenseman Larry Murphy rifled a pass toward Loney, which hit Broten's skate and bounced behind goalie Hayward just as Loney crashed into him for the game-clinching score.

Hayward was livid. "I was buried in the back of the net," the goalie stated after the game. "I'm not happy about that. I made a save, and I wound up in the back of the net."[3]

Be that as it may, the goal counted, and the Pens came away with the victory that had finally given them the edge in the series. They received a lengthy standing ovation from their frenzied, sweaty home crowd, which had seen their long-suffering team inch to within a victory of winning its first Stanley Cup.

BOX SCORE

Teams	1	2	3	F
Minnesota	1	1	2	4
Pittsburgh	4	1	1	6

Per	Team	Goal (Assist)	Time
1	Pittsburgh	Lemieux 15 (Murphy, Coffey)	5:36
1	Pittsburgh	Stevens 17 (Coffey, Murphy)	10:08
1	Pittsburgh	Recchi 9 (Lemieux, Bourque)	11:45
1	Pittsburgh	Recchi 10 (Lemieux, Murphy)	13:41
1	Minnesota	Broten 9 (Tinordi)	14:52
2	Minnesota	Gagner 11 (Propp)	6:54
2	Pittsburgh	Francis 6 (Mullen)	16:26
3	Minnesota	Dahlen 2 (Smith, Duchesne)	1:36
3	Minnesota	Gagner 12 (Propp, Gavin)	7:42
3	Pittsburgh	Loney 2 (Murphy, Francis)	18:21

Team	Goalie	Saves	Goals
Minnesota	Casey	9	4
Minnesota	Hayward	16	2
Pittsburgh	Barrasso	6	1
Pittsburgh	Pietrangelo	15	3

Shots	1	2	3	F
Minnesota	7	9	9	25
Pittsburgh	18	5	8	31

#48

The Perfect Month

When the Pittsburgh Penguins went on a record-setting 17-game winning streak in 1993, they technically didn't go through an entire month—with at least 10 games scheduled—unblemished. In fact, it's a feat that no NHL franchise had ever achieved, until March 2013, that is, when the Penguins had the opportunity to complete a perfect calendar month against the New York Islanders.

But the perfect month was not the record that the Pens or their fan base were focused on as the team took to the ice at the Consol Energy Center on this afternoon, because the Penguins were also challenging the '93 club's all-time record win streak.

Pittsburgh had begun the strike-shortened 2013 campaign with a solid but unspectacular 13–8 start. At that point, things began to jell as the club shook off the disappointment of the surprising six-game, first-round upset it had suffered at the hands of the Philadelphia Flyers in the playoffs the year before. After the loss, Pittsburgh general manager Ray Shero traded star center Jordan Staal to Carolina after he turned down their 10-year extension, and fans wondered if Pittsburgh could rebound and contend once again.

That question was answered as the team embarked on a 14-game winning streak that started on March 1 with an exciting 7–6 overtime win against the Montreal Canadiens. After giving up 17 goals during the first four games of the streak, the Penguins became more stable defensively. Marc-Andre Fleury and their most important free-agent signing, backup goaltender Tomas Vokoun, were spectacular, allowing only nine shots to get past them in the following 10 contests, three of which were shutouts, including the two games preceding the Islander contest on the 30th.

The team was now not only one game away from tying the league's second-best winning streak, set by the 1981–82 New York Islanders, but one game from finishing March with a perfect record. The streak was even more impressive considering that they had played an uncharacteristically high number of games in March since the league was trying to cram 48 contests into a four-month period following the strike. Despite the demanding schedule, Pittsburgh's hopes for a perfect month would be bolstered by Shero adding three impressive players at the trade deadline: defenseman Doug Murray, veteran left winger Brenden Morrow, and the prize of the trade deadline season, right winger Jarome Iginla from the Calgary Flames. On this night, the additions would turn out to be critical.

A Consol Energy Center record crowd of 18,673 was silenced just over a minute into the game when Pittsburgh captain Sidney Crosby was hit by an errant slap shot that tipped off the stick of defenseman Brooks Orpik and onto his chin. With blood pouring from his face, Crosby fell to the ice and was taken to a local hospital, where he had an operation to fix what turned out to be a broken jaw.

The sight of their fallen leader troubled the team, including Iginla, who was playing his first game in a Penguins uniform. "It's very tough to see that happen to anybody on the ice," he said, "but this is your teammate, and Sid's such a great player. It's a very, very unfortunate play."[1]

The Pens seemed to lose focus as they allowed the Islanders to fire a flurry of shots on goal before they were able to get one themselves. The streak seemed in jeopardy, but Pittsburgh had the hottest goalie in the league between the pipes. Vokoun, who had stepped in for the injured Fleury two games earlier, kept Montreal off the board in relief of Fleury in the first game, then shut out Winnipeg two days later. His sharpness continued against the Islanders as he turned aside eight straight New York shots to begin the game and 24 in the first two periods—including thwarting a five-on-three Islanders power play—as the teams battled to a scoreless tie entering the last period of regulation.

With the perfect month now in peril, the Penguin offense finally started to get in gear. Matt Cooke put the home team on the board midway through the frame when he pushed a rebound off a shot by defenseman Deryk Engelland past Islanders keeper Evgeni Nabokov to give Pittsburgh a 1–0 lead. Five minutes later the advantage increased to two when James Neal put a wrist shot behind Nabokov for his 18th goal of the year. Even without their captain, the

Penguins were proving they were still one of the best teams in the league, and the ecstatic crowd could taste a historic victory.

The excitement turned to trepidation as the Islanders continued to put pressure on Vokoun. Yet the Pittsburgh goalie was exceptional, turning away 35 New York shots and extending his scoreless streak to 162 minutes. More importantly, Vokoun had almost singlehandedly allowed the Penguins to continue their winning streak and reach a perfect 15-0-0 mark in March.

While the club did eventually lose to the Buffalo Sabres in its next game and soon after lost Crosby for the rest of the regular season, the win against the Islanders marked a monumental achievement, something no other franchise in the history of the game could claim.[2]

BOX SCORE

Teams	1	2	3	F
New York	0	0	0	0
Pittsburgh	0	0	2	2

Per	Team	Goal (Assist)	Time
3	Pittsburgh	Cooke 6 (Engelland, Kennedy)	8:10
3	Pittsburgh	Neal 18 (Malkin, Murray)	13:04

Team	Goalie	Saves	Goals
New York	Nabokov	25	2
Pittsburgh	Vokoun	35	0

Shots	1	2	3	F
New York	12	12	11	35
Pittsburgh	5	13	9	27

#47

It's a Great Day for Hockey

Most hockey fans point to the drafting of Mario Lemieux in 1984 as the moment the Penguins transformed from a long-suffering loser into a Stanley Cup champion. But a lesser-known series of events proved just as important—when owner Edward DeBartolo Sr. hired a talented triumvirate as the nucleus of his front office. First he tabbed Craig Patrick as his general manager, who in turn brought in arguably the greatest coach in NHL history, Scotty Bowman, to be his director of player personnel. Then on June 12, 1990, DeBartolo added the third and most significant component as head coach: Bob Johnson, who not only won three national championships at the University of Wisconsin but led the Calgary Flames to the Stanley Cup Finals in 1986.

Johnson seemed to be the perfect fit for a team that was long on potential but had yet to taste success in the postseason. "Badger Bob" proved to be a positive force on the entire team, and his attitude was infectious. "He was always in a good mood, and he put you in a good mood," Penguin winger Rob Brown once said. "He was bigger than life."[1]

The positive attitude would prove to be a precious commodity. Though Lemieux missed most of the season with a herniated disc, Johnson's Penguins found a way to win a division title for the first time in their 24-year history. Then with Lemieux back on the ice at season's end, Pittsburgh fought its way through the playoffs and ultimately won the Stanley Cup championship that most Penguin fans never thought would come.

Johnson was on top of the world. He would tell anyone who would listen that every day was a great day for hockey and, certainly after what he'd accomplished, you'd believe him. He was selected to coach the U.S. hockey team in the 1991 Canada Cup, and it appeared the sky was the limit for both Badger Bob and the Penguins.

While preparing the U.S. team for the upcoming tournament, Johnson encountered some serious medical issues. He was hospitalized in August for a brain aneurysm, and while in the hospital doctors found a brain tumor that was discovered to be malignant.

Back in Pittsburgh, the Penguins' assistants took over at first; then Bowman was tabbed to run the team behind the bench on an interim basis. Johnson tried to contribute from his hospital bed in Colorado Springs, but it proved too difficult, particularly when his condition worsened.

Finally on November 26, 1991, Bob Johnson passed away. The next night, his Penguins were scheduled to take on the New Jersey Devils at Civic Arena, a contest that turned into one of the most emotional experiences in the history of Steel City sports.

It began with a moving pregame ceremony honoring the fallen coach. The team formed a circle around center ice while the fans raised the battery-powered candles they were given before the game. The arena went dark and the scoreboard flashed the simple message: "Bob Johnson, 1931–1991." Linda Ronstadt's sad ballad "Goodbye, My Friend" played over the speakers.

It was a difficult moment for everyone in the arena, but particularly for Johnson's players. "It was really tough," center Ron Francis said afterward. "To see everyone in the stands with the lights up, knowing what kind of person Bob was. . . . It was very emotional for all of us."[2]

No one would have blamed the Pens for coming out flat in this game, but with Johnson's catchphrase "It's a great day for hockey" stenciled into the ice below them, the team was inspired and came out aggressively against the Devils.

With 10:04 remaining in the opening period, Francis danced around the New Jersey defense and blasted the puck between the pads of Devil goaltender Chris Terreri to send the Igloo crowd into hysterics and give Pittsburgh an early 1–0 lead. The Francis goal opened up the floodgates, as right winger Jamie Leach knocked in his first goal of the season, and grinding winger Phil Bourque made it 3–0 with a 35-foot slap shot past Terreri with 2:45 left in the first.

What looked like a blowout quickly turned into a tight game in the second period when New Jersey's Peter Stastny stole a clearing pass and scored in the first minute to make it 3–1. A minute later, Claude Vilgrain hit the net on a breakaway and cut the Penguin advantage to a goal. Devils winger Claude Lemieux (no relation to Mario) then knotted the contest midway through the period when he dribbled a shot toward Pittsburgh goalie Tom Barrasso, which the keeper accidently knocked into the net.

The emotional tidal wave that had carried the Penguins in the first period had now subsided. After building a comfortable lead, the Penguins appeared on their way toward losing the game intended to honor the man who led them to their only Stanley Cup.

Momentum shifted again late in the second period when Pittsburgh's Mark Recchi knocked in his own rebound on a power play to once again give the Pens the lead. Then in the third, Pittsburgh's Lemieux, who ended a two-game scoreless streak with an assist on Recchi's goal, set up defenseman Grant Jennings for a goal to make it 5–3.

After the Devils cut the lead to one, Pittsburgh regained some of its first-period fire as Paul Coffey restored the two-goal lead; then Lemieux netted a shorthanded tally to make it 7–4. Francis finished the scoring with his second goal of the game in the final seconds to seal the victory.

The sellout crowd stood and cheered the bereaved champions, but the true meaning of this emotional victory was not lost on either the players or the fans who witnessed it. Two days later, the team traveled to Colorado Springs to attend a memorial for Johnson and say their final goodbyes to the man who taught the Penguins how to win.

The lessons Johnson taught them continued to pay off throughout the 1991–92 campaign, as the Penguins honored their coach the best way they could: by winning a second consecutive Stanley Cup.

BOX SCORE

Teams	1	2	3	F
New Jersey	0	3	1	4
Pittsburgh	3	1	4	8

Per	Team	Goal (Assist)	Time
1	Pittsburgh	Francis 3 (Mullen, Roberts)	9:56
1	Pittsburgh	Leach 1 (Recchi)	11:18
1	Pittsburgh	Bourque 4 (Mullen, Roberts)	17:15
2	New Jersey	Statsny 13 (S. Stevens, Todd)	0:33
2	New Jersey	Vilgrain 5 (Weinrich)	2:07
2	New Jersey	C. Lemieux 17 (S. Stevens, Todd)	11:45
2	Pittsburgh	Recchi 9 (M. Lemieux, Coffey)	16:01
3	Pittsburgh	Jennings 2 (M. Lemieux, K. Stevens)	2:50
3	New Jersey	Richer 12 (Vilgrain)	6:25
3	Pittsburgh	Coffey 6 (Bourque, Mullen)	10:44
3	Pittsburgh	M. Lemieux 14 (Coffey)	15:39
3	Pittsburgh	Francis 4 (Coffey, Bourque)	19:55

Team	Goalie	Saves	Goals
New Jersey	Terreri	23	8
Pittsburgh	Barrasso	39	4

Shots	1	2	3	F
New Jersey	16	15	12	43
Pittsburgh	14	6	11	31

#46

PENGUINS 3, ST. LOUIS BLUES 1
OCTOBER 13, 1967

The Win Column

On February 1, 1930, Pittsburgh's entry in the National Hockey League, the Pirates defeated the Detroit Cougars at Duquesne Gardens. While any victory for this franchise that had struggled in its brief five-year history was noteworthy, no one could have anticipated the significance that triumph would ultimately carry.

It proved to be the Pirates' final win of the season, as they lost 15 of their last 16 games and tied one. Following the disappointing regular season, in which the club finished with a miserable 5–36–3 mark, the team's owners found themselves in dire financial straits following the stock market crash of 1929. The team moved to Philadelphia, and that victory against Detroit proved to be the last victory a Pittsburgh team would win in the NHL for nearly four decades.

After serving as the home to the American Hockey League Hornets, a group that included Pennsylvania state senator Jack McGregor, Pittsburgh Steelers owner Art Rooney, H. J. Heinz III, and Richard Mellon Scaife convinced the NHL's board of governors to include Pittsburgh as one of the cities granted a franchise as part of the six-team expansion for the 1967–68 season. And with that, the Penguins were born.

Though he'd never posted a .500 record in his four seasons at the helm of the New York Rangers, Red Sullivan was named the Penguins' first head coach and led the Pens onto the ice for the first time on October 11, 1967, losing to the Montreal Canadiens 2–1. Two days later they visited St. Louis to take on the Blues in hopes of logging the city's first NHL victory in 37 years.

The Penguins opened up the scoring at 8:18 of the first period. With the Blues' Fred Hucal in the penalty box, Pittsburgh right wing Paul Andrea took control of the puck behind the St. Louis net and sent a pass to left wing Ab McDonald, who fired a 25-foot slap shot past Blues goalie Seth Martin to give Pittsburgh a 1–0 lead.

St. Louis controlled the rest of the period, outshooting Pittsburgh 17–6, and Penguins goalie Hank Bassen stopped every shot but one, a soft shot that tied the game less than two minutes after McDonald's goal. The game continued as a closely fought affair until less than five minutes remained in the second period, when St. Louis defenseman Noel Picard was sent to the penalty box for holding. The Blues looked like they were going to successfully kill off the penalty, but then Penguins center Art Stratton knocked in a rebound of a Keith McCreary shot with one second left in the power play to give Pittsburgh a 2–1 lead.

With their inaugural victory in sight, the Pens played strongly in the third period, but gave the Blues an opportunity to tie the game when Pittsburgh's Al MacNeil put St. Louis on the power play with an elbowing penalty. Then Pittsburgh center Earl Ingarfield, whom the Penguins had selected with their first pick in that year's expansion draft, made the play of the game to secure the historic victory.

Ingarfield stole a pass and broke toward the St. Louis goal. The 33-year-old Alberta native faked a shot on Martin, sending the Blues' goalie off balance, then placed a shot just inside the post for a two-goal advantage with under 15 minutes left in the game.

The Penguins kept the pressure on, outshooting St. Louis 16–9 in the final period, and hung on for the 3–1 victory.

In the long run, there were several wins that may have had more drama or significance in the franchise's history, but to the patient hockey fans of the Steel City who had waited so long to see NHL hockey once again, it was a victory to be savored.

BOX SCORE

Teams	1	2	3	F
Pittsburgh	1	1	1	3
St. Louis	1	0	0	1

Per	Team	Goal (Assist)	Time
1	Pittsburgh	McDonald (Andrea, Bathgate)	8:18
1	St. Louis	Keenan (Schock, Arbour)	9:44
2	Pittsburgh	Stratton (McCreary, Ubriaco)	17:15
3	Pittsburgh	Ingarfield	5:59

Team	Goalie	Saves	Goals
Pittsburgh	Bassen	37	1
St. Louis	Martin	32	3

Shots	1	2	3	F
Pittsburgh	6	13	16	35
St. Louis	17	12	9	38

#45

Contenders

The first seven seasons of Pittsburgh Penguins hockey were filled with mediocrity. In that period, the team won only one playoff series and had never been considered a contender for the Stanley Cup. But all of that changed when general manager Jack Button hired Marc Boileau as head coach.

A native of Pointe-Claire, Quebec, Boileau had a 20-year professional hockey career, primarily in the minor leagues, before he arrived in Pittsburgh in February 1974 to take over a team that was enduring a dismal season. With a record of 14–31–5 when he arrived, the Penguins showed remarkable improvement, closing out the remainder of the season with a 14–10–4 mark.

The momentum continued the next season as the Pens went from doormat to contender, completing the 1974–75 campaign with 89 points, 16 more than their previous franchise high. It was a young, explosive team led by Jean Pronovost, Syl Apps, and 19-year-old rookie Pierre Larouche. They finished fourth in the league in scoring, tying an NHL record with nine players eclipsing the 20-goal plateau.

Pittsburgh's prize for its successful season was a spot in the preliminary round of the Stanley Cup playoffs against the St. Louis Blues in a best-of-three matchup. Since the National Hockey League had doubled its size through expansion in 1967, the Blues had been the most successful of the six new franchises, making the playoffs in six of their first seven seasons, including three appearances in the Stanley Cup Finals. They were led by center Gary Unger and 39-year-old goaltender Eddie Johnston (who 10 years later would be the Penguins' general manager who drafted Mario Lemieux).

The Penguins started off the brief series with an exciting 4–3 victory at

Civic Arena and then would travel to St. Louis two nights later with a chance to win their first playoff series since defeating the Oakland Seals in 1970.

Boileau chose 25-year-old Gary Inness as his starting goalie after Inness had enjoyed a fabulous sophomore season, winning 24 games, a Penguins record at the time, with a 3.09 goals-against average. The young goaltender was tested right away as the Blues came out strong, peppering Inness with several good scoring opportunities in the first period. Two minutes into the game, Blues veteran center Red Berenson—who went on to become the legendary coach at the University of Michigan—gave St. Louis an early lead, tapping in a rebound off his initial shot. Three minutes later, Pittsburgh's Pronovost pulled in a pass from Apps to tie the contest at one.

Tallying 14 shots on Inness in the opening period, St. Louis eventually took the lead after the Pens' defense blocked a Floyd Thomson shot that was directed in by the Blues' Bill Collins for a 2–1 advantage.

It looked like the home team would go into the locker room with the lead at the first intermission when the Blues' Pierre Plante was sent off the ice for interference. He then gave the Penguins a two-man advantage on the subsequent power play by not going directly to the penalty box. Despite the disadvantage, the Blues had just about killed the penalty when Pittsburgh defenseman Ron Stackhouse slid a soft shot past Johnston with only four seconds left on the power play to silence the sold-out arena. The fans were on their feet again minutes later when the Pittsburgh defense couldn't clear the puck out of their zone, and Larry Sacharuk rifled the go-ahead goal into the net to give the Blues a 3–2 advantage. Though St. Louis would continue to pressure Inness for the rest of the night, it would be the last time they beat him.

Pittsburgh gradually began to take control of the contest, first tying the game late in the second as Apps redirected a Lowell MacDonald shot, then forging ahead in the third. With Pittsburgh's Dave Burrows in the penalty box and St. Louis trying to once again go on top, rookie defenseman Colin Campbell broke in on the veteran goalie and beat Johnston for a 4–3 Penguin advantage. "I got control, but Johnston was blocking my angle," Campbell said after the game. "I waited until he hit the ice before I could shoot. I thought I was going to blow my big chance."[1]

He didn't, and the one-goal lead held until 35-year-old left winger Vic Hatfield ripped a 40-foot shot past Johnston with under four minutes left to make it 5–3 and clinch the game—and the series—for Pittsburgh. The Penguins and their fans received even more good news when, thanks to some other series upsets, they would have home-ice advantage in the quarterfinals against a young New York Islander squad.

The momentum from the unexpected victory over St. Louis carried over, as Pittsburgh raced to a three-game lead in the best-of-seven series with New York, only to see everything fall apart in four straight losses. It marked only the second time in the history of the NHL (and all North American pro sports leagues, for that matter) that a team had rallied from a 3–0 deficit to win a seven-game series.

While the epic collapse may be what most remember about the 1974–75 Penguins, lost in its impact was the team's emergence as a Stanley Cup contender for the first time in its brief history—exemplified by a rousing playoff victory over the favored St. Louis Blues.

BOX SCORE

Teams	1	2	3	F
Pittsburgh	2	1	2	5
St. Louis	2	1	0	3

Per	Team	Goal (Assist)	Time
1	St. Louis	Berenson (Sacharuk, Unger)	2:12
1	Pittsburgh	Pronovost (Apps, Campbell)	5:36
1	St. Louis	Collins (Thomson, Merrick)	9:15
1	Pittsburgh	Stackhouse (Arnason, Kelly)	17:56
2	St. Louis	Sacharuk (Patrick, Larose)	11:26
2	Pittsburgh	Apps (Mac Donald, Stackhouse)	14:27
3	Pittsburgh	Campbell (McManama)	4:23
3	Pittsburgh	Hadfield (Shock)	16:12

Team	Goalie	Saves	Goals
Pittsburgh	Inness	39	3
St. Louis	Johnston	24	5

Shots	1	2	3	F
Pittsburgh	10	10	9	29
St. Louis	14	14	14	42

#44

PENGUINS 9, ST. LOUIS BLUES 2
OCTOBER 15, 1988

The Greatest

For seven seasons, Wayne Gretzky had a stranglehold on the annual NHL scoring title with no one even close enough to offer a challenge. That streak ended in the 1987–88 season, when the Penguins' Mario Lemieux led the league with 168 points to finally snap Gretzky's string. He overtook Gretzky partially because of his own emerging greatness but also because Gretzky had suffered a knee injury that sidelined him for 16 games—almost a quarter of the season. Lemieux's mission in the 1988–89 campaign was to prove he truly had supplanted Gretzky as the best in the game. And Lemieux's performance on October 15, 1988, against the St. Louis Blues made a convincing argument that he had.

By 1988, Pittsburgh had begun to build a powerful offensive team around Lemieux. Paul Coffey, the highest scoring defenseman in the history of the game, was in his first full season in Pittsburgh, while Rob Brown and Dan Quinn had become two of the most dangerous scorers in the NHL. Looking to continue their momentum from their first plus-.500 season in eight years, Pittsburgh showed off their offensive prowess winning two of their first three games in the 1988–89 campaign while scoring 19 goals. While impressive, their defense had been essentially nonexistent in those first three contests, surrendering 19 to their opponents.

The Pittsburgh defense slipped early in its fourth contest as well, as the Blues scored on a three-on-two break 22 seconds into the game when Pittsburgh defenseman Rod Buskas awkwardly fell down. While it was an inauspicious beginning, it would quickly be forgotten as Lemieux soon took over the game.

After Pittsburgh's Steve Dykstra scored his only goal of the season on a pass from Jim Johnson, tying the contest midway through the opening period,

Lemieux would have a hand in every Penguin goal for the rest of the evening.

First, Lemieux and Quinn set up Brown for his third goal of the year, giving the Pens a 2–1 lead. Four minutes later, Lemieux and Bob Errey put defenseman Zarley Zalapski in position to score his third goal in four games.

While the offense was once again playing at a high level, the defense—showing a dramatic improvement in killing penalties—shut down the Blues after the opening-minute miscue. Pittsburgh goalie Steve Guenette appreciated the defensive effort in front of him, which allowed only 11 shots over the final two periods. "After their second goal, I was a spectator," the goalie recalled. "And I had a great seat."[1]

The second St. Louis goal cut the margin to 4–2 after Lemieux scored Pittsburgh's fourth goal himself early in the second period. Before the period was over, Lemieux set up Brown for a power-play goal, and less than a minute later, the game became a rout as Lemieux notched his second goal of the game to make it 6–2.

With 20 minutes still to play, Lemieux had already enjoyed a fabulous evening, notching two goals and five points. But in the third period, his nice game turned into a record-breaking performance.

Pittsburgh increased its advantage to five when Lemieux set up Robbie Brown for the first hat trick of Brown's career. And while Brown celebrated his achievement, he knew it wouldn't have happened without the talents of his center. "He's so smart," Brown said of Lemieux. "He knows what to do with the puck. It doesn't matter if there are six guys between us. You know he will get you the puck."[2]

With time running out, it looked like Lemieux would end the game by matching his own personal high of six points in a single contest. But with just over two minutes left, he eclipsed it, finding Errey with one of the terrific passes that Brown spoke of, making it 8–2.

Then, with just under a minute left, Lemieux feathered a pass to John Cullen on a power play, and Cullen put a shot past St. Louis goalie Vincent Riendeau to round out the scoring of what proved to be a historic evening.

The last assist gave Lemieux a team-record six assists and eight points for the game—making him just the 10th player in NHL history to record the achievement and just two points shy of the NHL record. His 13 points in his last two games vaulted him from 14th place to the top of the league's scoring race, a position he held onto for the remainder of what would be a marvelous season. He finished the 1988–89 campaign with 199 points, beating a fully healthy Wayne Gretzky by 31 and showing the hockey world he truly had become the greatest in the game—a transition that began with his one-man show on a historic October evening against the Blues.

BOX SCORE

Teams	1	2	3	F
St. Louis	1	1	0	2
Pittsburgh	3	3	3	9

Per	Team	Goal (Assist)	Time
1	St. Louis	Paslawski 4 (Cavallini, Benning)	:22
1	Pittsburgh	Dykstra 1 (Frawley, Johnson)	9:31
1	Pittsburgh	Brown 3 (Lemieux, Quinn)	11:19
1	Pittsburgh	Zalapski 3 (Errey, Lemieux)	15:19
2	Pittsburgh	Lemieux 5 (Bodger, Zalapski)	1:54
2	St. Louis	Hull 4	5:59
2	Pittsburgh	Brown 4 (Lemieux, Quinn)	7:55
2	Pittsburgh	Lemieux 6 (Brown, Dykstra)	8:59
3	Pittsburgh	Brown 5 (Lemieux)	7:23
3	Pittsburgh	Errey 2 (Lemieux, Buskas)	17:39
3	Pittsburgh	Cullen 1 (Coffey, Lemieux)	19:40

Team	Goalie	Saves	Goals
St. Louis	Riendeau	26	9
Pittsburgh	Guenette	20	2

Shots	1	2	3	F
St. Louis	11	7	4	22
Pittsburgh	11	7	17	35

#43

PENGUINS 2, OAKLAND SEALS 1
APRIL 8, 1970

The Postseason Waters

The Pittsburgh Penguins have enjoyed many memorable playoff encounters, four of which resulted in them hoisting Lord Stanley's cup, hockey's ultimate prize. But in 1970, their playoff résumé was empty, a canvas that had yet to be painted as they waded into postseason waters for the first time in franchise history.

The 1969–70 Penguins were an unspectacular club, finishing 12 games under .500 while ranking 10th out of 12 NHL clubs in offense and eighth in defense. Led by a pair of 37-year-old players, Dean Prentice and Ken Schinkel, Pittsburgh had the good fortune of residing in the NHL's Western Division, which included all six of the expansion franchises that had joined the league two years before. Despite their less-than-stellar record, the Penguins finished in second place in the weak division and secured a playoff spot.

While the Pens' roster was still loaded with veterans from the expansion draft, they were starting to add young talent into the mix. Jean Pronovost was a 24-year-old right winger who was purchased from the Boston Bruins and had scored 20 goals during the 1969–70 campaign. Another key addition was left winger Michel Briere, a 20-year-old third-round draft pick who finished third on the team with 45 points and looked to be headed toward stardom.

This youthful duo gave the team hope, and the future began with a best-of-seven western division semifinal matchup against the fourth-place Oakland Seals, who also contained a cadre of unimpressive castoffs and youthful players.

A marginal crowd of just 8,051 was on hand at Civic Arena, including several members of the defending world champion New York Mets, who had played a game against the hometown Pirates at Forbes Field earlier in the day. Before the crowd had time to settle into their seats, talented Oakland defenseman Carol Vadnais had been sent to the penalty box for hooking Briere. Six seconds later, Pronovost took a pass from Bob Woytowich and put a shot into the pads of Seals goalie Gary Smith, then pushed the rebound past him to give Pittsburgh an early 1–0 lead.

Not long after, Oakland scored a power-play goal to knot the score and was poised to take the lead late in the first period before Pittsburgh goalie Les Binkley made a spectacular save with his leg to keep the game tied. Binkley's play proved more and more important as the night wore on, and the contest remained a 1–1 stalemate until the final minutes.

With both goalies at the top of their games, it looked like the contest would go to overtime until a controversial play with just over seven minutes remaining. The Pens' Glen Sather took the puck from his own end and skated through the Oakland defense. He passed to center Wally Boyer and zipped past him looking for a return pass, but Oakland's Bert Marshall checked Sather, who flew into Oakland goalie Smith. Pens right winger Nick Harbaruk took the puck and slid it into the empty goal to give Pittsburgh the lead at 2–1.

Smith protested vigorously to referee Bruce Hood that he was interfered with, but Hood ruled that Sather was checked into Smith and upheld his decision.

With time running out and his team now trailing, Seals coach Fred Glover pulled Smith as Oakland put an extra attacker on the ice. The desperate Seals pressured Binkley in the last two minutes of the contest, but the Pens' goalie held firm and the Penguins emerged with an exciting victory.

Pittsburgh went on to sweep Oakland in four games before losing to the St. Louis Blues in six for the Western Division championship. Despite the fact they fell short in making the Stanley Cup Finals, their memorable postseason debut served as a dazzling first chapter in what would be a rich playoff history.

BOX SCORE

Teams	1	2	3	F
Oakland	1	0	0	1
Pittsburgh	1	0	1	2

Per	Team	Goal (Assist)	Time
1	Pittsburgh	Pronovost 1 (Woytowich, Morrison)	1:05
1	Oakland	Ehman 1 (Loughton, Roberts)	9:26
3	Pittsburgh	Harbaruk 1 (Boyer, Sather)	12:47

Team	Goalie	Saves	Goals
Oakland	G. Smith	34	2
Pittsburgh	Binkley	28	1

Shots	1	2	3	F
Oakland	13	9	14	36
Pittsburgh	6	13	10	29

#42

Backs Against the Wall

The 1994–95 NHL season had been a strange one. A players' strike wiped out almost half the season, and though each team played an abbreviated 45-game schedule, it provided plenty of excitement.

In the Northeast Division, the Penguins and Quebec Nordiques engaged in a spirited battle that saw Quebec win the division title by a narrow four-point margin. With the two teams notching the highest point totals in the conference, most figured one of them would wind up playing for the Stanley Cup. Surprisingly, in the first round of the playoffs, Quebec was upset by the conference's lowest seed, the New York Rangers, while the Pens faced their own unexpected troubles against the underdog Washington Capitals, who soared to a three-games-to-one advantage in their best-of-seven series on the strength of back-to-back blowouts in the third and fourth games in the nation's capital. The Penguins had to win Game Five at Civic Arena or begin a sudden and early vacation.

While the Pittsburgh defense would continue the ineffective play that had haunted the team throughout the series, with their backs against the wall, the strength of the team, the offense, would shake off its own struggles to save the season.

Penguins coach Eddie Johnston tabbed goalie Ken Wregget, who had played most of the abbreviated regular season while starter Tom Barrasso was recovering from a wrist injury, to start this contest. Yet early on he looked no more effective than Barrasso had been, allowing a pair of first-period goals as the Caps skated to an early lead. With Pens left winger Rusty Fitzgerald in the penalty box for high sticking late in the opening period, it looked like Pittsburgh was about to be blown out for the third consecutive time.

One of the hallmarks of a great hockey player is the ability to rise to the occasion when his team most needs him, and with the Penguins facing elimination, Jaromir Jagr proved that he was indeed one of the best in the game. Shorthanded, Jagr took the puck into the Capitals end, made a magnificent move around center Joe Juneau, and put a backhanded shot over the shoulder of Washington goaltender Jim Carey to pick up the Pens, cutting the deficit to one. With momentum now on their side, the Penguins quickly tied the game early in the second period when left winger Kevin Stevens rammed a shot past Carey, sending the sellout throng into a frenzy.

Despite the goal, the Caps hung tough through the momentum shift and the contest settled into a back-and-forth affair, with Washington continually taking one-goal leads only to see the Penguins quickly tie the score again. It started when Hunter scored four minutes after Stevens had tied it to make the score 3–2; then Pittsburgh's future Hall of Famer Ron Francis tied it at three, beating Carey through traffic.

The score held up until early in the third period when Washington's Peter Bondra closed in on Wregget on a two-on-one break after Penguin defenseman Ulf Samuelsson was late getting back into his defensive zone. Bondra slipped a shot past Wregget to put the Capitals ahead, 4–3.

Over the next two minutes, the Pittsburgh faithful leaped from ecstasy to agony. Moments after the Caps took the lead back, Jagr beat Carey for his fifth goal of the series to make it 4–4. Just 26 seconds later, Bondra netted his second goal of the game to once again give the Capitals a one-goal advantage with time—and the Penguins' opportunities—running out.

Just as the thwarted Civic Arena fans began to wonder if their team might have one more comeback in it, Stevens would answer them with a resounding yes. The left winger took a pass from Francis and scored on a backhander to tie the contest for the fourth time.

The established rhythm of the contest dictated that Washington would score the next goal to win the game and the series, but the Pens began working from another script. The Pens were inspired after referee Mike McGeough ignored a high stick by the Capitals' Michal Pivonka, which cut Pittsburgh tough man Kjell Samuelsson—a penalty that would have given Pittsburgh an automatic five-minute power play. "That, to me, is a deliberate attempt to injure," Johnston noted after the game.[1]

The missed call rankled and motivated the team over the final minutes of regulation, setting up an unlikely hero to set up the game-winning goal of overtime. Francois Leroux, who had only two assists during the regular season, uncharacteristically pushed the puck into the offensive zone. He found Luc Robitaille with a perfect pass, and Robitaille then finished the play with his fourth goal of the series to give the Penguins a hard-fought victory. "For a minute there," Robitaille said of Leroux, "when he beat his guy to the corner, I thought he was Mario."[2]

The victory brought the once-despondent Penguins back to life in the series, narrowing their deficit to one game and sparking a dramatic turnaround. Pittsburgh outscored Washington 10–1 in the next two games to secure a come-from-behind series triumph and a trip to the conference semifinals—which had seemed nearly impossible prior to their Game Five heroics.

With their backs against the wall, the Pens had found new life, postponing the summer vacation that only days before had seemed imminent.

BOX SCORE

Teams	1	2	3	OT	F
Washington	2	1	2	0	5
Pittsburgh	1	2	2	1	6

Per	Team	Goal (Assist)	Time
1	Washington	Hunter 3 (Jones)	11:19
1	Washington	Johansson 3 (Miller)	15:36
1	Pittsburgh	Jagr 4 (Francis, K. Samuelsson)	17:13
2	Pittsburgh	Stevens 3 (Francis, Murphy)	5:57
2	Washington	Hunter 4 (Juneau, Jones)	9:27
2	Pittsburgh	Francis 2 (Murphy, Stevens)	15:42
3	Washington	Bondra 4 (Khristich)	7:14
3	Pittsburgh	Jagr 5 (Francis)	8:23
3	Washington	Bondra 5 (Cole)	8:49
3	Pittsburgh	Stevens 4 (Francis, Jagr)	11:42
OT	Pittsburgh	Robitaille 5 (Leroux)	4:30

Team	Goalie	Saves	Goals
Washington	Carey	29	6
Pittsburgh	Wregget	23	5

Shots	1	2	3	OT	T
Washington	11	10	7	0	28
Pittsburgh	8	10	12	5	35

PENGUINS 5, NEW YORK ISLANDERS 0
NOVEMBER 21, 2011

The Concussion

Until recent years, recovering from a sports-inflicted concussion was a simple process. A coach or trainer asked the athlete how many fingers he was holding up or what city he was in. If the athlete answered correctly, he was deemed to be ready to play.

Throughout most of the history of sport, no one knew just how dangerous concussions were. With medical research came answers—not only of the severity of head injuries but how they had devastated the postcareer lives of many athletes, even leading to premature death.

On January 1, 2011, the sports world was focused on Heinz Field in Pittsburgh, where the Penguins were hosting the Washington Capitals in the NHL's marquee regular-season event, the Winter Classic. It was a day meant to celebrate not only the game and the team but the city itself, yet the celebration was quickly forgotten when the game was being defined by a questionable hit that would cost the Penguins their captain.

Late in the second period, Washington's Dave Steckel delivered an aggressive blindside hit to the head of Pittsburgh's Sidney Crosby. While Crosby appeared to be injured, he stayed in the game to play one shift in the third period before sitting out the final minutes. Four days later, Tampa Bay defenseman Victor Hedman drove Crosby into the boards head first. Once again Crosby persevered, playing the rest of the game. But it quickly became apparent something was wrong.

He accompanied the team on a flight to Montreal for its next game but continued to suffer from concussion-like symptoms and was held out of the game. Crosby, who was enjoying the best start of his career with 32 goals and 66 points at the season's midpoint, was expected to miss only a week, but if it had been just 10 years earlier, he probably would have been back on the ice within a day or two. Luckily for Crosby, doctors were now aware of how serious head injuries were and proceeded with caution before permitting him back on the ice. In Crosby's case, a week proved to be very wishful thinking as the odyssey of his injury, and subsequent recovery, dominated the local headlines for the second half of the season.

The week off the ice turned into more than two months before the young star could even return to practice. And even then, the question of when he would return to game action continued to be the subject of debate and rumors by the press and fans alike.

As it turned out, Crosby wouldn't play for the rest of the season, and not long after the team was eliminated from the playoffs, it was announced that his injury was far more serious than originally thought. The questions soon turned to not *when* Crosby would return, but *if*.

Speculation continued until early November, 11 months after the concussion, when the team announced what Penguin fans had longed to hear, that Sidney Crosby would finally put on his uniform and play against the New York Islanders.

As number 87 emerged onto the Consol Energy Center ice on November 21, 18,571 rabid Pens fans roared and rose to their feet to offer a rousing ovation. Just that he was able to resume his career was a victory in itself, yet he wasn't satisfied with just being on the ice. He wanted to prove that he was still one of the best players in the game. The show he would put on that night did exactly that.

It didn't take long for Crosby to thrill the sellout crowd as he broke through the Islander defense and put a backhand shot past New York goalie Anders Nilsson to give Pittsburgh a 1–0 lead five minutes into the game. It was his first goal in 328 days. Before the first period was over, he also displayed his tremendous playmaking skills, feeding defenseman Brooks Orpik, who rifled a shot over Nilsson to put Pittsburgh up by two.

Inspired by the return of their captain, the Pens continued the onslaught in the second period. Crosby garnered his second assist of the game when he set up Evgeni Malkin for his sixth goal of the young campaign, and the lead swelled to 4–0 just over two minutes later when Steve Sullivan took a perfect Malkin pass and sent it past Nilsson.

The game was well in hand, but Crosby wasn't done, beating the beleaguered New York goalie with a backhand shot for his second goal of the game and the final touch on a memorable 5–0 victory.

While it was a tremendous moment for Crosby, the celebration of his return was fleeting. Eight games into his comeback, he was hit by an elbow to the head, putting him out of action for nearly four more months. Crosby did eventually return on March 15 against the Rangers and luckily was able to remain healthy the rest of the season.

Through all the adversity he'd faced in his career, his dramatic first comeback performance against the Islanders proved that Sidney Crosby was still one of the best players in the NHL—and one of the most memorable ever to don a Penguins uniform.

BOX SCORE

Teams	1	2	3	F
New York	0	0	0	0
Pittsburgh	2	2	1	5

Per	Team	Goal (Assist)	Time
1	Pittsburgh	Crosby 1 (Dupuis, Engelland)	5:24
1	Pittsburgh	Orpik 2 (Crosby, Dupuis)	16:29
2	Pittsburgh	Malkin 6 (Letang, Crosby)	3:17
2	Pittsburgh	Sullivan 2 (Malkin, Neal)	5:53
3	Pittsburgh	Crosby 2 (Dupuis, Michalek)	2:06

Team	Goalie	Saves	Goals
New York	Nilsson	31	5
Pittsburgh	Fleury	29	0

Shots	1	2	3	F
New York	9	11	9	29
Pittsburgh	12	15	9	36

PENGUINS 5, MONTREAL CANADIENS 2
JANUARY 26, 1997

Le Magnifique

"Le Magnifique" is how the rabid hockey fans of Montreal described a young hometown legend by the name of Mario Lemieux.

Drafted at the age of 15 by the Laval Voisons of the Quebec Major Junior Hockey League, Lemieux quickly showed the rare talent that he was. He scored 562 points in three years, including a remarkable 282 in the 1983–84 season before the Penguins drafted him the following year. While Montreal fans had to struggle with the reality that one of their own would thrill crowds 400 miles away in Pittsburgh, they were comforted by the fact that on January 26, 1997, he would perform one of his most magnificent feats in front of them at Montreal's brand-new Molson Centre.

By 1997, Lemieux had been in the league 12 seasons and was winding down. Though his career had been affected by a myriad of medical maladies, including chronic back pain, tendonitis, a herniated disc, and a battle with Hodgkin's lymphoma, he'd fought through to place his name among the legends of the game. He led the league in scoring and was named NHL MVP three times while guiding Pittsburgh to a pair of championships.

While only 31, it was rumored he would retire at the end of the season, though he was leading the league in scoring. Most assumed this game in late January would be his last in his hometown. And he turned in one of his greatest performances.

Montreal had always been a tough trip for the Penguins, who'd won only four of 64 games on the Canadiens' home ice in their history, but Pittsburgh got off to a quick start. Pens rookie goaltender Patrick Lalime—unbeaten in his last 15 starts—stopped 14 Montreal shots in the first period, some in a spectacular manner. But one got past him off the stick of defenseman David Wilkie to give Montreal a 1–0 lead.

Though Pittsburgh lost defenseman Frederick Olausson for the game when a slap shot broke his cheekbone early in the game, Lalime was up to the challenge. He was at his best midway in the second period when he stopped former Pens sniper Mark Recchi twice on breakaways in a 15-second span.

While Montreal was dominating the action, Pittsburgh was able to tie things up early in the second period when defenseman Jason Woolley scored a power-play goal. Though Montreal had rifled 29 shots on goal by the end of the period, the score remained 1–1 going into the third.

Though he remained scoreless, Lemieux's game picked up in the second period with several remarkable plays. He had two golden opportunities to score but missed an open-net shot and then hit the post on another. But in the third period, the Penguin captain came alive.

His record-setting performance started at the 4:35 mark when he picked up a rebound off a shot by teammate Ron Francis and sent it past Montreal goalie Jocelyn Thibault to give the Pens a 2–1 lead. Five minutes later, Lemieux scored a spectacular goal from behind the net when he banked the puck off Thibault and into the goal, stretching the Pens' advantage to 3–1.

After Montreal's Sebastien Bordeleau made it 3–2, Lemieux once again showed his magnificence with a breakaway backhanded shot to restore the two-goal lead. It gave Mario the 39th hat trick of his career, which tied him with Mike Bossy for second place in NHL history behind Wayne Gretzky.

While scoring a hat trick in his hometown was a spectacular enough achievement, Lemieux wasn't done. With time running out, he took his performance to a level that only 11 other NHL players had ever reached. With 30 seconds on the clock, Lemieux sent a shot nearly the length of the ice into the empty net for a record-tying fourth goal in a single period, clinching a 5–2 Pittsburgh victory. The Montreal fans, even in defeat, truly appreciated what they had seen and offered their hometown hero a thunderous standing ovation at the end of the game.

Lemieux did indeed retire at the end of the season (though would return to the ice three years later), making this night in Montreal one of the truly remarkable moments of his spectacular career. It was a night in which he proved the nickname of Le Magnifique was fitting.

BOX SCORE

Teams	1	2	3	F
Pittsburgh	0	1	4	5
Montreal	1	0	1	2

Per	Team	Goal (Assist)	Time
1	Montreal	Wilkie 4 (Tucker, Thornton)	8:59
2	Pittsburgh	Woolley 4 (Francis, Nedved)	3:56
3	Pittsburgh	Lemieux 31 (Francis, Jagr)	4:35
3	Pittsburgh	Lemieux 32 (Mullen, Nedved)	9:06
3	Montreal	Bordeleau 1 (Savage, Baron)	12:42
3	Pittsburgh	Lemieux 33 (Francis)	16:54
3	Pittsburgh	Lemieux 34	19:29

Team	Goalie	Saves	Goals
Pittsburgh	Lalime	42	2
Montreal	Thibault	33	4

Shots	1	2	3	F
Pittsburgh	11	13	14	38
Montreal	15	14	15	44

#39

PENGUINS 5, NEW YORK RANGERS 2
APRIL 13, 2016

Goalie Number 3

In the 2014 Stanley Cup playoffs, the Pittsburgh Penguins had appeared to be on a run to a Stanley Cup championship, defeating the Columbus Blue Jackets before rolling to a three-games-to-one lead in the Eastern Conference semifinals against their hated rivals the New York Rangers. Who knew that they were about to collapse?

The goals stopped as the Penguins were outscored 10–3 in the remaining three contests to lose the series, which cost general manager Ray Shero and coach Dan Blysma their jobs. They never quite rebounded, just barely qualifying for the playoffs a year later when they faced these same Rangers in the first round. Once again they fell to New York, losing in five close games as they kept Pittsburgh off the scoreboard for most of the series, allowing only eight goals in the five contests.

As the 2016 campaign came to a close, the Penguins had apparently turned things around and were playing better than any other team in the league. Unfortunately, as the Pens became successful again, they suffered injuries to their top two goalies with both Marc-Andre Fleury and Matt Murray out with concussions, the latter of which came in a meaningless contest during the final game of the season against the Flyers.

Widely criticized for playing what appeared to be his starting playoff goalie in a game that meant nothing only to see him injured, coach Mike Sullivan was forced to play the team's third string goaltender, Jeff Zatkoff, against the club that had been their ultimate nemesis the previous two seasons.

This was the same kind of hard luck that had followed the team over the past couple years. They led the NHL in man games lost to injury with 479 in 2013–14, and while they had lowered that number two years later to 279, ninth

45

in the circuit, Malkin was hurt late in the season before they took another blow when Fleury was hit in the mask on March 31 off the stick of former teammate James Neal, which caused his second concussion of the season.

Having one of the best campaigns in his illustrious NHL career, Fleury had a spectacular 2.29 goals-against average and a .921 save percentage—oftentimes the only reason the Penguins were in the playoff hunt following a dismal start offensively in the season. Fortunately, they wouldn't miss a beat as rookie Matt Murray continued the stellar play in goal.

A third-round pick in the 2012 entry draft out of Sault Ste. Marie, Murray was thought of as the goalie of the future. After a fast start at Wilkes-Barre, that future came much earlier than expected when Fleury's injury proved to be more serious than anticipated. He went 9–2–1 down the stretch with a 2.00 GAA and an even more impressive .931 save percentage. Murray was ready to lead the team in the playoffs until his predecessor returned. Wanting to keep him sharp, Sullivan let the young rookie start in the regular season finale against the Flyers. Late in the first period, he was hit in the head by the leg of Philadelphia winger Brayden Schenn as he was skating through the crease. Murray was helped into the locker room and did not return.

It was hoped that one of the Pens' top two goalies would be ready for action when it came time to take on the Rangers, but as game time approached it became apparent that Sullivan would have to call on goalie number 3, Zatkoff, who had been inactive for 52 days before playing against the Flyers.

A former Miami (OH) goalie, Zatkoff had been praised by his former NCAA coach for his ability to keep the team loose; he had confidence Zatkoff would excel in this situation. "He's grateful for the opportunity he has in the NHL and he's ready to do what he needs to do. That's why guys love him and play for him," coach Enrico Blasi stated. Penguins Nick Bonino concurred, calling the third stringer a "glue guy"[2] for keeping the players loose and together with his sense of humor.

Regardless of the intangibles that Zatkoff brought to the team, this was a good New York Ranger club, despite the fact they struggled down the stretch. Having the Penguins third-string goalie in net certainly would negate the home ice advantage Pittsburgh had earned. What the Rangers did not count on was the fact the 2015–16 Pittsburgh Penguins were a resilient bunch and Zatkoff was about to have the game of his life.

Early on, the game looked no different from the previous two playoff encounters with the Rangers dominating play. Luckily, Pittsburgh's third stringer was playing his best and kept the game scoreless with several spectacular saves as time was running out in the first. At that point, the bad luck changed sides as New York's Mark Staal somehow had the butt of his stick find a hole in goaltender Henrik Lundqvist's mask, hitting his eye and sending their all-star goaltender to the ice writhing in pain—a one in a million shot that put the momentum of this game squarely in the Penguins' favor.

Lundqvist got up and remained in the contest, but Patric Hornqvist slipped a rebound past the injured net minder with 18 seconds left in the opening frame to give Pittsburgh a 1–0 advantage. Lundqvist was evaluated in the locker room and the decision was made to pull him in favor of New York's backup goalie Antti Raanta.

Outshooting the Pens 10–7 in the second period, New York kept the game close and with it the chance to keep their four-game Consol Center winning streak alive. Unfortunately for the Rangers, Pittsburgh once again scored late in the period when Hornqvist found Sidney Crosby streaking in on Raanta alone. Number 87 flipped a wrist shot over the Ranger goalie's glove with 1:04 remaining in the second for a two-goal cushion.

Looking comfortable, the Penguins put themselves in a precarious position with penalties that gave New York a two-man advantage early in the third. Derek Stepan made Pittsburgh pay, beating Zatkoff to cut the Pens' lead back to one.

A year ago this might have caused Pittsburgh to stumble, but this team just shook off the goal and quickly turned a close game into a one-sided affair. A little over two minutes later Thomas Kunhackl netted a shorthanded goal to help Pittsburgh reestablish its two-goal lead before Hornqvist tipped a loose puck in the Ranger crease at 8:02 to make it 4–1.

Stepan proved to be New York's only offense with his second goal halfway through the period, but the Pens' defense held firm the rest of the way as Hornqvist completed his hat trick late in the game with an empty net goal that sealed an impressive 5–2 victory.

The third string netminder, who stopped 35 of 37 shots, was thrilled but knew the next game would be another challenge. "I'll enjoy it tonight, but, you know, get focused on Game 2 and I just continue to work hard no matter what happens. You can't predict what's going to happen."[3]

While the Rangers would rebound and defeat Zatkoff and the Penguins 4–2 three days later, it was this game that showed their rivals that this year would be different. Pittsburgh dominated the final three games to win this first-round matchup in five games. It was the beginning of their Stanley Cup run, a run that may not have happened without the Game One heroics of goalie number 3.

BOX SCORE

Team	1	2	3	F
New York	0	0	2	2
Pittsburgh	1	1	3	5

Per	Team	Goal (Assist)	Time
1	Pittsburgh	Horqvist 1 (Sheary, Letang)	19:42
2	Pittsburgh	Crosby 1 (Hornqvist)	18:56
3	New York	Stepan 1 (Nash, Brassard) PP	3:10
3	Pittsburgh	Kuhnhackl 1 (Bonino, Letang) SH	5:31
3	Pittsburgh	Horqvist 2 (Kessel, Crosby) PP	8:02
3	New York	Stepan 2 (Boyle, Zuccarello)	10:11
3	Pittsburgh	Horqvist 3 (Daley, Crosby) EN	17:10

Team	Goalie	Saves	Goals
New York	Lundqvist	10	1
New York	Raanta	16	3
Pittsburgh	Zatkoff	35	2

Shots	1	2	3	T
New York	12	10	15	37
Pittsburgh	11	7	13	31

#38

PENGUINS 5, BOSTON BRUINS 1
MAY 23, 1992

Wales Squared

Facing the Boston Bruins in the 1991 Wales Conference Championship Series, the Penguins rallied from a two-game deficit to win four straight contests and clinch their first trip to the Stanley Cup Finals.

Twelve months later, they would face Boston again at the same stage of the playoffs, but many things had changed. The Penguins were now the defending league champions and had built one of the most powerful offensive lineups in league history. They also came into the postseason with the experience and know-how necessary to win a championship. On the other hand, they also served as a much bigger target for the Bruins to try to avenge their defeat the year before.

Led by future Hall of Fame defenseman Raymond Bourque and Czecho-slovakian sharpshooter Vladimir Ruzicka, the Bruins were coming off an uncharacteristically mediocre regular season, finishing with only 84 points. As disappointing as it was, their campaign was still good enough for second place in the Adams Division and a postseason berth for the 25th consecutive year. The Bruins then caught fire in the playoffs, knocking off Buffalo and Montreal to set up a rematch with Pittsburgh.

The Bruins were overwhelmed though by the Penguins, who skated to a narrow victory in Game One and then blowouts in the second and third contests to take a commanding lead in the series. Pittsburgh entered Game Four just one victory away from its second straight Stanley Cup appearance in what had already been a difficult and emotional season.

In addition to losing head coach Bob Johnson after a battle with brain cancer, two of the most important players from the Pens' championship run the year before—Paul Coffey and Mark Recchi—were both dealt away at the trade deadline. Not surprisingly, Pittsburgh struggled in the regular season as well as the first two rounds of the playoffs.

The Penguins finally began to regain their championship form in Game Four of the division finals against New York, which began a six-game winning streak that propelled them to the brink of another conference championship. Center Ron Francis felt that the adversity they faced ultimately helped bring them together. "We certainly had a lot of adversity," he said. "And I don't think we handled it very well at first. But it's the sign of a good hockey club when you learn to handle adversity well. And we learned."[1]

The lessons they learned continued from the onset as Jaromir Jagr gave them a quick 1–0 lead five minutes into the game with a backhander past Bruin goalie Andy Moog. Not long after, Mario Lemieux scored one of the most memorable and breathtaking goals of his illustrious career when he stole a pass at his own end, then—although the Pens were shorthanded at the time—took the puck through the Boston defense and pushed it past Moog for the goal. It was a stellar moment for the Penguins' captain, who had missed part of the Ranger series and the first game of the conference finals after being slashed by New York's Adam Graves. The goal also amazed his opponents. "It's almost scary," Boston's Dave Poulin said. "It looks like he's toying with you, like he can turn it on at any moment. That's how good he is. When he's out there, he creates so much room for the other guys. He opens things up for them."[2]

The Bruins trailed 2–0 at the first intermission and were lucky it wasn't worse. Jagr had a second goal disallowed when referee Don Koharski blew the whistle right as Jagr and a couple Bruin defensemen ran into the net, knocking the cage off its moorings seconds before the puck crossed the goal line, while Kevin Stevens hit one off the post. Even with the missed opportunities, the Pens continued to dominate the game, opening up a three-goal advantage early in the second when defenseman Paul Stanton took a perfect pass from Francis and sent it past Moog for the score. Lemieux then all but ended the Bruins' hopes with another impressive goal, skating past Boston defenseman Larry Murphy, stopping in front of the Boston goalie, and stuffing it past him.

Pittsburgh right wing Dave Michayluk and Boston's Stephen Leach each scored meaningless goals in the third period, but the game had long been decided by that point.

Unlike the year before, when Pittsburgh broke tradition and hoisted the conference championship trophy (the accepted superstition in the NHL is to not touch a team trophy until the club can lift the Stanley Cup), this time the players just looked at it, knowing that their work was far from done. "It's not like we're done yet," said center Bryan Trottier. "There's one more level, one more notch."[3]

Indeed, a Stanley Cup Finals matchup against Chicago lay just ahead, but for now the Penguins had extended an unpredictable season with a familiar achievement: winning a Wales Conference championship with a victory over Boston.

BOX SCORE

Teams	1	2	3	F
Pittsburgh	2	2	1	5
Boston	0	0	1	1

Per	Team	Goal (Assist)	Time
1	Pittsburgh	Jagr 9 (Francis, Stanton)	4:51
1	Pittsburgh	Lemieux 10	13:09
2	Pittsburgh	Stanton 1 (Francis, McEachern)	5:27
2	Pittsburgh	Lemieux 11 (Tocchet)	13:58
3	Boston	Leach 4 (Carpenter, Oates)	5:53
3	Pittsburgh	Michayluk 1 (Callander, Hrdina)	19:49

Team	Goalie	Saves	Goals
Pittsburgh	Barrasso	29	1
Boston	Moog	20	5

Shots	1	2	3	F
Pittsburgh	9	10	6	25
Boston	7	13	10	30

PENGUINS 6, ST. LOUIS BLUES 2
APRIL 2, 1972

Long Odds

The path to the Penguins' second trip to the playoffs in their brief five-year history was clear, if not easy on the final day of the regular season: they needed to beat a strong St. Louis Blues team and then hope the Philadelphia Flyers would lose to the Buffalo Sabres, who had one of the worst records in the NHL.

While the Pens didn't have the odds on their side, they'd already defied expectations over the previous month just to get to this point.

On March 8, Pittsburgh lost to the Montreal Canadiens, while the Flyers also picked up a victory and then another the following evening to give them 57 points to the Penguins' 51 with 11 games left. The chances of Pittsburgh making up that ground in so little time were slim, at best.

With many writing them off, the Penguins started playing their best hockey of the season. They went undefeated over the next five games with a 2–0–3 mark while the Flyers were 0–3–1 during the same time period. By March 23, Pittsburgh had caught up to Philly, and both teams were tied with 58 points. The Flyers bounced back, and after the teams skated to a 4–4 tie in the second-to-last contest, Philadelphia held a two-point lead over Pittsburgh.

While the Flyers had the easier matchup in the finale, the Pens did hold the tiebreaker over Philadelphia after winning the season series with the Flyers, 3–2–1. If the teams ended the season with the same number of points, it would be Pittsburgh that got the nod for the final playoff spot.

A boisterous standing-room-only crowd of 13,100 shook the roof off the Igloo as the Penguins took the ice in a must-win game against St. Louis. After an early first-period goal by the Blues' Phil Roberto, who ripped a 20-foot slap shot past Penguin goalie Jim Rutherford, Pittsburgh started to take control of the game.

Pens center Syl Apps found Val Fonteyne with a pass, and Fonteyne took the puck behind the Blues net before he fed a perfect pass to Nick Harbaruk, who put a pinpoint shot into the net to tie the score. Two minutes later, Pittsburgh's Greg Polis tipped in an Al McDonough shot for a power-play goal and a 2–1 Penguin advantage at the end of one.

As good as the Pens had played toward the end of the first period, initially it appeared as though it wouldn't matter. Word trickled in from Buffalo that Philadelphia's Bobby Clarke had scored his 35th goal of the year to give the Flyers a 1–0 lead at the end of the first period.

Knowing there was nothing they could do about the outcome in Buffalo, the Pens concentrated on the task at hand. Once again they were able to quickly piece together two goals, and within two minutes, Pittsburgh had increased its advantage to three. McDonough found Eddie Shack for a score to make it 3–1; then, while playing a man down, Fonteyne made another beautiful pass through the St. Louis defense to Ron Schock, who scored his 16th goal of the campaign to increase the Pens' lead.

With time running out in the second period and the Civic Arena crowd celebrating, things turned quiet quickly. First, Roberto scored his second goal of the game with nine seconds left to cut the Penguin lead to 4–2, followed by the news from PA announcer Beckley Smith that the Flyers led the Sabres 2–1 at the end of two.

Despite the late goal from Roberto, Pittsburgh rebounded and made quick work of St. Louis in the third period. Forty-seven seconds into the last frame, Duane Rupp was set up perfectly by Fonteyne and Apps to score his fourth goal of the season to give the Pens back their three-goal lead. Two minutes later, Fonteyne continued his fabulous evening by sending a rebound off a Harbaruk shot past Blues goaltender Ernie Wakely to make it 6–2, Pittsburgh.

The Penguin defense was impenetrable the rest of the way, keeping St. Louis from making it any closer, but the sellout throng was not paying much attention to the game in the Igloo, but rather to what was happening in Buffalo. Just when it appeared the Flyers were certain to clinch a playoff spot, Buffalo tied the score at two with 11 minutes left. A tie would do the Penguins no good, and as the clock ticked down under a minute in Buffalo, it appeared the Flyers would hang on for a stalemate and hold off the charging Penguins. Then lady luck decided to shine upon Pittsburgh. With less than 10 seconds left and an empty net behind him, Buffalo right wing Mike Byers passed the puck to teammate Gerry Meehan, who beat Philadelphia's Doug Favell with only four seconds remaining to put Buffalo in front for the first time.

As the final seconds ran down in Buffalo, Smith was given the chance to make the announcement of a lifetime as he informed the Penguin faithful the Sabres had won and the Pens had successfully beat the long odds to earn a postseason bid. What was once considered an improbability was now reality: a date against the Chicago Blackhawks in the Stanley Cup playoffs, secured by an impressive late-season stretch, a memorable victory in the season finale, and a little bit of good fortune.

BOX SCORE

Teams	1	2	3	F
St. Louis	1	1	0	2
Pittsburgh	2	2	2	6

Per	Team	Goal (Assist)	Time
1	St. Louis	Roberto 14 (Murphy, Unger)	10:29
1	Pittsburgh	Harbaruk 12 (Fonteyne, Apps)	14:14
1	Pittsburgh	Polis 3 (Apps)	16:19
2	Pittsburgh	Shack 16 (Mc Donough, Pronovost)	11:35
2	Pittsburgh	Schock 16 (Fonteyne)	15:12
2	St. Louis	Roberto 15 (Unger, Murphy)	19:51
3	Pittsburgh	Rupp 4 (Fonteyne, Apps)	0:47
3	Pittsburgh	Schock 17 (Harbaruk)	2:47

Team	Goalie	Saves	Goals
St. Louis	Caron	22	2
St. Louis	Wakely	14	2
Pittsburgh	Rutherford	29	2

Shots	1	2	3	F
St. Louis	11	7	13	31
Pittsburgh	19	8	15	42

#36

PENGUINS 12, WASHINGTON CAPITALS 1
MARCH 15, 1975

The '62 Mets Revisited

Occasionally, extremely bad sports franchises can be as legendary as the champions we all remember so fondly. Many baseball fans, for instance, know as much about the 120-loss 1962 New York Mets, often considered the worst team in modern baseball history, as they do about the dominant New York Yankees teams of the 1940s and '50s.

There are many debates over the greatest team in modern NHL history, but when it comes to the worst, the discussion begins and ends with the expansion 1974–75 Washington Capitals.

The numbers to defend this claim are staggering, beginning with an 8–67–5 mark good enough for an all-time NHL low .131 winning percentage. The Caps finished last in goals scored and last in goals allowed—in fact, the 446 goals they surrendered was the worst tally in league history. At one point, Washington lost 17 straight games and wound up losing 39 of its 40 road contests. For as bad as the Capitals were that year, when they visited Civic Arena to play the Pittsburgh Penguins that March, they made "bad" look even worse.

It was Game 12 of their record-setting 17-game losing streak, and former Penguin coach Red Sullivan—the second of three unfortunate head coaches tapped to guide the Caps through this miserable campaign—chose goaltender Michel Belhumeur, who would finish the year winless at 0–24–3, to face the high-scoring Pens over starter Ron Low. As it happened, both would play (and play poorly) in a game in which Pittsburgh set a handful of franchise records, some that still stand more than four decades later.

While the Capitals were limping toward the finish line, the Penguins were enjoying the best season to date in their short history. They had built an offensive juggernaut based on a balanced scoring attack that included nine players who eclipsed the 20-goal plateau . . . six of whom would score on this evening.

The onslaught started early and never ended. Pittsburgh center Syl Apps began the festivities a minute into the game, taking a pass from Colin Campbell and sending a shot past Belhumeur to make it 1–0. Pittsburgh quickly netted two more goals as 19-year-old rookie phenom Pierre Larouche scored his 25th of the year 90 seconds later, and then Rick Kehoe notched his 27th at the 6:37 mark, giving the Pens a three-goal advantage.

The beleaguered Capitals' defense briefly stopped the bleeding by holding Pittsburgh scoreless for the next six minutes, but then the floodgates opened once again. Lowell MacDonald notched his 25th goal, followed by defenseman Barry Wilkins's fifth in a quick three-minute stretch to give the Pens a 5–0 lead at the end of the first period that saw them launch 19 shots on goal. And they were just warming up.

The Caps enjoyed their lone highlight of the evening when they netted the opening goal of the second period, but the Pittsburgh offense continued its dominance by peppering Belhumeur for 19 more shots and three goals over the next 20 minutes as Vic Hadfield, "Battleship" Bob Kelly, and Bob McManama all scored, increasing the Penguin advantage to 8–1 at the second intermission.

With victory in hand, the Penguins eased off the throttle a bit in the third period, but against a team like this, it made little difference. Within a minute, the Penguins hit double digits when Hadfield and Larouche both notched their second goals of the game to make it 10–1. The deluge soon continued as the Penguin offense persistently fired good shots on goal, now tended by Low, at a record pace. Kehoe soon scored his second goal, then Lew Morrison set a new team record for goals in a game when he scored the Penguins' 12th of the evening. With a record 27 shots on goal in the final 20 minutes, it was as dominant a period as the Pens had ever played, before or since. For the game, the Washington goalies faced a whopping 65 shots from a Pittsburgh attack that smelled blood in the water.

The Penguins set six records that night, including most shots (65), assists (20), and individual players' points (32) in a game (32), as well as for largest margin of victory. True, they may have been recorded against the NHL's version of the '62 Mets, but that the marks still stand 40 years later underlines the historic significance of the Penguins' dominance that night.

BOX SCORE

Teams	1	2	3	F
Washington	0	1	0	1
Pittsburgh	5	3	4	12

Per	Team	Goal (Assist)	Time
1	Pittsburgh	Apps 23 (Wilkins, Campbell)	1:02
1	Pittsburgh	Larouche 25 (Wilkins, Arnason)	2:38
1	Pittsburgh	Kehoe 27 (Hadfield, Schock)	6:37
1	Pittsburgh	Mac Donald 25 (Apps, Pronovost)	12:24
1	Pittsburgh	Wilkins 5 (McManama, Paradise)	14:45
2	Washington	Labre 4 (Lynch, Bailey)	3:21
2	Pittsburgh	Hadfield 26 (Kehoe)	3:45
2	Pittsburgh	Kelly 23	5:59
2	Pittsburgh	McManama 3 (Wilkins, Inness)	15:15
3	Pittsburgh	Hadfield 27 (Kehoe, Schock)	2:30
3	Pittsburgh	Larouche 26 (Wilkins, Kelly)	3:26
3	Pittsburgh	Kehoe 28 (Schock, Hadfield)	8:32
3	Pittsburgh	Morrison 4 (McManama)	11:14

Team	Goalie	Saves	Goals
Washington	Belhumeur	30	8
Washington	Low	23	4
Pittsburgh	Inness	23	1

Shots	1	2	3	F
Washington	7	10	7	24
Pittsburgh	19	19	27	65

#35

PENGUINS 4, NEW YORK ISLANDERS 3
MAY 11, 2013

Breaking the Islanders' Jinx

Many franchises—in many sports—have one particular rival that seemingly always delivers heartbreak. The Pittsburgh Penguins have had bigger rivals and rivalries in their history, but arguably no team has caused them as much misfortune as the New York Islanders.

While the Penguins hold the lead in the all-time regular-season series between the teams, it's been a very different story in the postseason. Prior to 2013, the teams had met in the playoffs three times, and in every series, the Islanders pulled out a victory in the deciding game each time the series went to the final and deciding game with the Penguins looking to make history.

In 1975, Pittsburgh blew a three-games-to-none lead in a first-round series as the Islanders won four straight to become just the second North American professional sports team to rally from such a deficit to win a seven-game series. Seven years later, it was the Penguins who staged a comeback, rebounding after losing the first two games of a best-of-five first-round series to force Game Five. After skating to a 3–1 lead, the Penguins allowed a pair of New York goals in the final five minutes and then lost the contest in overtime. In the 1993 playoffs, the teams met again, and once more the Islanders emerged victorious, pulling off an upset over the back-to-back Stanley Cup champions.

Twenty years later, the teams would square off for a fourth postseason battle—eerily similar to their previous playoff encounter. Pittsburgh was the prohibitive favorite to win it all in 2013 after posting the best regular-season winning percentage in franchise history, while the upstart Islanders had just barely squeaked into the playoffs, snagging the eighth and final spot.

The Penguins opened up the series with a commanding 5–0 victory, which most assumed was a preview of a Pittsburgh series romp. But then the "Islander

Jinx" seemed to kick in as the Penguins squandered an early lead in Game Two and lost as the series evened. Despite being outplayed, the Pens managed to pull out a narrow overtime victory on the road in the third game but then were defeated again two days later as the Islanders knotted the series at two games apiece. The teams headed back to Pittsburgh with momentum firmly in New York's corner and Pens fans on the verge of panic, dreading a fifth playoff series defeat to the Islanders.

The Penguins seemed to finally take control of the series with a dominant win in Game Five, just like they had in 1993, but now would have to travel back to Nassau Coliseum and the Islanders' home ice to try to end the series and avoid yet another decisive contest. Nightmares of past playoff series between these two teams materialized in the heads of Penguin fans everywhere.

Any momentum Pittsburgh acquired in its previous victory evaporated quickly in Game Six as the Islanders dominated play from the outset. Pittsburgh goaltender Tomas Vokoun, whom coach Dan Bylsma inserted before Game Five to replace the struggling Marc-Andre Fleury, kept the game close despite several great New York scoring opportunities. Continually beating the Penguins to the puck, the Islanders took the lead a little over five minutes into the game when Josh Bailey put a perfect pass on John Tavares's stick in the face-off circle to the left of Vokoun, and Tavares flipped a shot past the Pittsburgh goalie to make it 1–0. Despite being outplayed, the Pens tied the contest two minutes later as Jarome Iginla stuffed a Sidney Crosby rebound into the net underneath Evgeni Nabokov. But, cashing in on their aggressive play, the Islanders surged back ahead with a goal in the final minute of the first period.

Though New York was playing its best hockey of the series while the Penguins were playing their worst—reflected by the Islanders' 16–6 shots-on-goal advantage in the second period—Pittsburgh again managed to tie the game. Joe Vitale took the puck into the New York end and found Pascal Dupuis, who flipped the puck into the net for his fifth goal of the series.

Again, Pittsburgh's reprieve was short-lived, as the Islanders crept to a 3–2 advantage early in the third period, and as the clock ticked down, it appeared the Islander hex would continue, and a seventh game would be necessary.

New York kept pressuring the Pens to attempt to create a two-goal cushion, but Vokoun hung tough, keeping Pittsburgh in the game long enough for Malkin to make the play of the game. Skating into the Islanders' end one-on-four, he shot a pass to defenseman Paul Martin, who beat Nabokov to tie the game with only 5:16 left.

Regulation ended, and the teams went into overtime, evoking memories of past heartbreaks at the hands of the Islanders. But rather than mirroring the disappointing postseason history between the two clubs, the time had come for the Penguins to write their own story and break away from the heartbreak of the past. And fittingly, the most unlikely of players would be the one to do it.

Brooks Orpik had played in 77 postseason contests in his career without ever scoring a goal. But that was no surprise since scoring was not his specialty, reflected by his going scoreless in 2013 and only setting off the horn 11 times in 10 NHL seasons. His first playoff goal, though, would be a memorable one.

The Islanders had several great chances in overtime but were rebuffed by Vokoun each time. Finally, with almost eight minutes gone in the extra session, Malkin got to a loose puck and sent it to Tyler Kennedy. Kennedy passed the puck to Orpik, who launched a slap shot toward Nabokov. The puck went over the New York goalie, hitting the crossbar before settling over the goal line to end the game and send the Penguins to the second round of the playoffs for the first time in three years.

More importantly than advancing to the next round, Orpik's goal finally ended a jinx that had been torturing the franchise for 38 years.

BOX SCORE

Teams	1	2	3	OT	F
Pittsburgh	1	1	1	1	4
New York	2	0	1	0	3

Per	Team	Goal (Assist)	Time
1	New York	Tavares 3 (Bailey, Carkner)	5:36
1	Pittsburgh	Iginla 2 (Crosby, Martin)	7:39
1	New York	McDonald 2 (Aucoin, Grabner)	19:23
2	Pittsburgh	Dupuis 5 (Vitale, Niskanen)	10:59
3	New York	Grabner 1 (Aucoin)	2:21
3	Pittsburgh	Martin 1 (Malkin)	14:44
OT	Pittsburgh	Orpik 1 (Kennedy, Malkin)	7:49

Team	Goalie	Saves	Goals
Pittsburgh	Vokoun	35	3
New York	Nabokov	17	4

Shots	1	2	3	OT	T
Pittsburgh	7	6	6	2	21
New York	12	16	7	3	38

PENGUINS 6, WASHINGTON CAPITALS 2
MAY 13, 2009

No Comparison

Comparing the best players in various sports has long been a favorite debate among fans. There are countless permutations, like Magic Johnson vs. Larry Bird in the NBA, Joe Montana vs. Dan Marino in the NFL, and Ted Williams vs. Joe DiMaggio in Major League Baseball. Similar comparisons have been made between great NHL players over the years, one of the more recent being the Pittsburgh Penguins' Sidney Crosby vs. the Russian star from the Washington Capitals, Alex Ovechkin. With the 2009 Stanley Cup playoffs in full swing, these two players had a unique opportunity to prove their claim as their respective teams engaged in a tough seven-game Eastern Conference semifinal series.

Both Crosby and Ovechkin had finished the regular season ranked among the top three in the league in scoring, with Ovechkin finishing second in points with 110 and being the only player in the NHL to eclipse the 50-goal plateau that season with 56. Crosby was seven points behind his Washington rival but showcased his tremendous playmaking skills with 70 assists, second in the league.

While defeating Crosby in their individual statistical race, Ovechkin's team also held an advantage over Crosby's as Washington won the Southeastern Division with 108 points while the Pens finished second in the Atlantic with 99.

With comparable stars leading equally matched teams, it was no surprise that the first six games of the series were tightly fought affairs, with each team winning three. Washington had started out by winning the first two games, with Ovechkin scoring four goals, including a hat trick in the second contest, but the Penguins responded by winning the next three before the Capitals stayed alive with an exciting overtime victory in Game Six to force a decisive seventh game.

In the series, five contests were decided by one goal, and for 92 percent of the minutes played in the series, the teams were within one goal of each other. Game Seven would be played at Washington's Verizon Center, and Ovechkin, who had been spectacular in the series so far with seven goals and 13 points, looked to clearly separate himself from Crosby by sending the Penguins back to Pittsburgh to begin their off-season. Crosby, meanwhile, had other plans.

Seven minutes into the game, the Pens' captain began what would be an unexpected onslaught when he scored his 11th goal of the playoffs to give the Pens a 1–0 lead. By contrast, eight seconds later, Craig Adams scored his first playoff goal in 42 career postseason games to increase the Pens' lead to two.

Then, in the first two minutes of the second period, the Penguins all but ended the series. Crosby started it off by sending a perfect pass to 38-year-old veteran Bill Guerin, who scored 28 seconds into the period to make it 3–0. Just 1:44 later, Kris Letang scored to put Pittsburgh in front by four goals, prompting Capitals coach Bruce Boudreau to pull goalie Semyon Varlamov in favor of Jose Theodore.

The goalie change did not stop the Penguin onslaught, as Jordan Staal directed a pass from Miroslav Satan past Theodore for an even more comfortable five-goal cushion.

In the first Game Seven of his career, Crosby played remarkably, thoroughly overshadowing Ovechkin, who suffered through his worst game in the series. "[Crosby] won't say he likes front and center, the big stage, or anything like that," Guerin said after the game. "But he really knows how to perform in it."[1]

Alexander the Great, as Capitals fans called Ovechkin, scored late in the second period to bring his team back to within four, but it was too little, too late for the Capitals. Moments later at the other end, Crosby put the topping on his magnificent performance by stealing a pass and scoring for his second tally of the game to make it 6–1. Washington added a meaningless goal later in the period, and the Penguins rounded out a satisfying 6–2 victory.

When the two superstars met at center ice for the traditional post-series handshake, Ovechkin said that he "wished him good luck, and told him to win the Stanley Cup."[2]

Crosby would do just that, further staking his claim in the debate over who was the better player in the game.

BOX SCORE

Teams	1	2	3	F
Pittsburgh	2	3	1	6
Washington	0	1	1	2

Per	Team	Goal (Assist)	Time
1	Pittsburgh	Crosby 11 (Gonchar, Malkin)	12:36
1	Pittsburgh	Adams 1 (Fedotenko, Orpik)	12:44
2	Pittsburgh	Guerin 5 (Crosby)	0:28
2	Pittsburgh	Letang 3 (Malkin, Satan)	2:12
2	Pittsburgh	Staal 2 (Satan)	11:37
2	Washington	Ovetchkin 11	18:09
3	Pittsburgh	Crosby 12	2:02
3	Washington	Laich 3 (Fleischmann)	6:36

Team	Goalie	Saves	Goals
Pittsburgh	Fleury	19	2
Washington	Varlamov	14	4
Washington	Theodore	10	2

Shots	1	2	3	F
Pittsburgh	16	8	6	30
Washington	5	7	9	21

#33

Bonino, Bonino, Bonino

The Punjabi people are made up of Indo-Aryans who originated in a region called the Punjab, meaning land of five waters, which was located in Pakistan and northern India in the eighteenth century. Today there are over 125 million Punjabi people, 431,000 who live in Canada. Some of the favorite sports for the Punjabi people include chess and carrom. In Canada they add hockey to their list of sports they are passionate about, even producing a version of the famed *Hockey Night in Canada* that is broadcast to the Punjabis. It was a broadcast that went relatively unknown in North America until the 2016 Stanley Cup playoffs when it and the Penguins Nick Bonino crossed paths, turning both into unsuspecting stars.

A talented two-way center from Boston University, Bonino became the sixth-round pick of the San Jose Sharks, who then traded his rights to Anaheim where he immediately started in the NHL. As an NHL player, he never amounted to much before signing with Neumarkt/Egna of the Italian League during the lockout in 2012–13 and scored 26 goals in 19 games. The confidence he gained in Italy seemed to turn his career around after the strike was settled, netting a career-high 22 goals for the Ducks a year later.

Ending up with Vancouver in 2014–15, which ironically is one of the epicenters of the Canadian Punjabi people, Pittsburgh would acquire the center with defenseman Adam Clendening and a second-round pick for third-line center Brandon Sutter. It was hoped he would replace Sutter's production, but early on that didn't seem to be happening. After scoring three goals in the first month of the season, it was almost four more months before he would get his fourth. Things got better for the Hartford native in the final month of the campaign as he became part of what would become a very effective HBK line with Carl Hagelin and Phil Kessel as Bonino scored six times. As good as it was, no one ever could have imagined the star status that was just around the corner for the former Duck.

He went goalless in the opening round against the Rangers but contributed five assists. He finally got on the scoreboard in the first game in their next series against the 2016 President Cup–winning Washington Capitals. Bonino netted a goal in the 4–3 overtime loss that gave the Caps their only advantage of the series.

To say Washington had a less than stellar history in the playoffs against Pittsburgh was an understatement. They faced each other eight times, with the Pens ending up with series victories on seven occasions. This one seemed different for the Caps as they entered the 2016 Stanley Cup playoffs. Having the best record in the league, the Capitals were considered the strongest team in franchise history. With a one-game advantage in the Eastern Conference semifinals their long-awaited cup seemed only a few weeks away. Unfortunately, like they had so many times in the past, Pittsburgh came up with an inspired performance winning three of the next four contests to send the series into a sixth game at the Consol Center with a chance to end the Capitals season for an eighth time.

While preparing to broadcast the contest, Punjabi play-by-play man Harnarayan Singh saw on his sheet that they had Nick Bonino listed on his line sheet under all three positions; while he certainly found it odd, he had no idea at the time that seeing that would inspire him to be a hockey celebrity, especially after the Pens blew a 3–0 lead in the game partially because Bonino was given a penalty for delay of game after flipping the puck out of bounds at an inopportune time.

Even though they had a three-games-to-two lead, the pressure may have been squarely on the Penguins in this contest. They lost the fifth game, 3–1, and if they couldn't emerge victorious in their home arena, it would force a seventh and deciding contest on Washington's home ice; early on it was apparent that Pittsburgh would have no talk of a return to the nation's capital

Phil Kessel started the scoring early in the first period by snapping a 43-foot shot past the Capitals All-World goaltender Braden Holtby for a 1–0 lead. They then threatened to make it a rout in the second after former Pen Brooks Orpik was sent off for a double minor after a high stick against Patric Hornqvist. Within 33 seconds, Kessel netted his second with a 12-foot wrist shot before Carl Hagelin tipped in a shot from Olli Maata to make it a three-goal cushion. Against the Toronto Maple Leafs, a three-goal lead in the second is safe; against the President Cup winners, it was anything but.

It was a good sign that Pittsburgh's struggling power play woke up against the Capitals in the second, troublesome that the Caps also did the same. T. J. Oshie of Olympic fame as well as the Penguins' nemesis in the first game of the series, beat Matt Murray with only a minute and a half left in the second to cut the lead to two.

Having a 44–0 mark with a lead after the second period would give comfort to most, but when Washington's Justin Williams beat Murray from 12 feet out to make it 3–2 the sellout crowd in the Consol Center became very nervous. It was at this point one of the strangest, yet unluckiest sequences in Pittsburgh Penguin history occurred. First, Chris Kunitz was sent to the penalty box for a delay of game after flipping the puck over the glass. Then a minute and six seconds later Bonino did the same thing, giving Washington a two-man advantage. The Pens were playing very well shorthanded as Kunitz returned to the ice. It was at that point, remarkably, that Ian Cole did the same thing two seconds after Kunitz returned. Trying to hold off such a talented team for such a long period of time with two men off the ice was too much for Pittsburgh to handle; 27 seconds later, Washington tied the game scoring on a slap shot by John Carlson.

With the three-goal lead evaporated, their Stanley Cup dreams had just taken a hit. Washington now had the momentum, and a seventh game was looking more likely. This was a different Penguins team, though, from the previous few years, a resilient team that displayed their new character, keeping the Capitals off the board the remainder of the third to force overtime. When they came out for the extra period, Pittsburgh became the dominant team.

They were getting to the loose pucks and creating chances. Early in the overtime, Hornqvist appeared to have won the game with a shot that got past Holtby, but Jay Beagle dove on his belly to keep the shot out of the goal. At 6:32 the Caps wouldn't be so lucky when a Hagelin shot came off the Washington goalie in front of the net. Bonino came rushing in and Punjabi announcer Singh was ready to make his now legendary call. The Pens winger directed it in behind Holtby, ending the game and the series. An excited Singh screamed "Bonino the goal" four times before letting out a long B-O-N-I-N-O-O-O-O-O-O. It was a call that quickly went viral.

It made what was a memorable moment legendary in team lore and also helped both Singh and Bonino become national stars as the Penguins once again ended Washington's championship hopes.

BOXSCORE

Team	1	2	3	OT	F
Washington	0	1	2	0	3
Pittsburgh	1	2	0	1	4

Per	Team	Goal (Assist)	Time
1	Pittsburgh	Kessel 4 (Dumoulin, Hagelin)	5:41
2	Pittsburgh	Kessel 5 (Letang, Kunitz) PP	7:05
2	Pittsburgh	Hagelin 4 (Maata, Daley) PP	7:38
2	Washington	Oshie 6 (Backstrom, Ovechkin) PP	18:30
3	Washington	Williams 3 (Backstrom)	7:23
3	Washi Ngton	Carlson 5 (Williams, Ovechkin) PP	13:01
Ot	Pittsburgh	Bonino 2 (Hagelin, Kessel)	6:32

Team	Goalie	Saves	Goals
Washington	Holtby	38	4
Pittsburgh	Murray	36	3

Team	1	2	3	OT	T
Washington	10	8	18	3	39
Pittsburgh	11	12	12	7	42

PENGUINS 4, CAROLINA HURRICANES 1
MAY 26, 2009

Cowher Karma

The residents of Raleigh, North Carolina, were used to dealing with adverse weather and storm warnings, but in the spring of 2009, Carolina hockey fans were downright panicked as they came face-to-face with Hurricane Penguin.

A red-hot Pittsburgh team had coasted to a three-games-to-none lead in the Eastern Conference Finals and was on the brink of ending an otherwise promising season and exciting playoff run for the Carolina Hurricanes. In an effort to change the momentum and get karma on its side, Carolina turned, ironically, to a Pittsburgh sports legend to help save the season.

The Penguins, after grinding out a tough six-game victory over Philadelphia and then a tight seven-game encounter with Washington, had held off a Carolina rally in Game One of the conference finals for a 3–2 victory and then scored a combined 13 goals in their next two games to coast to a commanding series lead.

Entering what could be its final game of the season, Carolina was desperately trying to reverse its fortunes. The front office even convinced former Pittsburgh Steelers head coach Bill Cowher—a former North Carolina State football player and current North Carolina resident—to sound the ceremonial siren that greets the Hurricane players as they took the ice. It was an act that was considered treason in Pittsburgh as Penguin fans universally criticized the former Steel City icon for what, to many, was aiding and abetting a Pittsburgh opponent.

The karmic gamble appeared to pay off early when the Hurricanes' Eric Staal scored his 10th goal of the playoffs, and first in this series, only 1:36 into the game to give Carolina the early 1–0 advantage.

Coach Paul Maurice, who took over 25 games into the season and led the Hurricanes to a 33–19–5 mark, had his troops playing aggressively as they continually beat the Pens to loose pucks. Momentum was clearly on the side of the home team, but then karma switched direction.

Almost seven minutes after Staal gave Carolina the lead, Pittsburgh's Ruslan Fedotenko tipped in a Philippe Boucher slap shot to tie the game at one. Then, just before the first period ended, a fluke play seemed to take the steam out of the Hurricanes' Stanley Cup run. The Penguins' Max Talbot flipped a wrist shot from the point toward Carolina goalie Cam Ward, who was 5–0 lifetime in elimination games and had never lost a playoff series. Unfortunately for both Ward and Carolina, Hurricane defenseman Anton Babchuk deflected the puck over Ward and into the net to give the Pens a 2–1 lead. "It hit [Babchuk's] skate, popped up, and I lost sight of it for a split second," the Carolina goalie said after the game. "Bad break, fluke goal."[1]

Babchuk, who was playing his first game of the series, soon made another blunder that led to Pittsburgh's third goal. An errant pass onto the stick of the Penguins' Bill Guerin started a two-on-one break with Sidney Crosby that ended with Guerin slipping the puck past Ward for a two-goal advantage.

With his team's proverbial back already to the wall, Maurice knew the Hurricanes' defense could not give up another goal. "We just talked about staying in [the game] as long as we possibly could," he said afterward. "You're down one, you're down two. We didn't want to get it to three."[2]

That's exactly what happened though. With time running down and Carolina desperately trying to get back into the game, Pittsburgh's Craig Adams—who hadn't scored in his first 42 playoff games but had netted three in the past five—tallied an empty-net goal to secure the Penguins' second consecutive trip to the Stanley Cup Finals.

The possibility of a season-saving victory that had seemed so promising earlier in the evening had instead descended into karma gone bad. Apparently, the magic that Cowher brought to the Steel City in football just didn't carry over to Raleigh—or hockey.

BOX SCORE

Teams	1	2	3	F
Pittsburgh	2	1	1	4
Carolina	1	0	0	1

Per	Team	Goal (Assist)	Time
1	Carolina	Staal 10 (Cole, Samsonov)	1:36
1	Pittsburgh	Fedotenko 6 (Boucher, Talbot)	8:21
1	Pittsburgh	Talbot 4 (Satan)	18:31
2	Pittsburgh	Guerin 7 (Crosby)	12:10
3	Pittsburgh	Adams 3	18:50

Team	Goalie	Saves	Goals
Pittsburgh	Fleury	30	1
Carolina	Ward	21	3

Shots	1	2	3	F
Pittsburgh	9	10	6	25
Carolina	5	16	10	31

#31

The Igloo

For a half century, one of the most unique sites in the city of Pittsburgh was an oddly configured arena that resembled an igloo more than a sports arena; hence the nickname it ultimately acquired.

The Civic Arena, eventually renamed Mellon Arena (after Mellon Financial purchased the naming rights in 1999) was more than just a strange-looking piece of architecture in the Hill District. It was an American original.

The facility, which was the oldest in the NHL during its final season, was constructed out of 3,000 tons of steel produced from the Pittsburgh mills. Apart from resembling an Eskimo's home, its most memorable feature was a retractable roof that was anchored by a 260-foot-long cantilevered arm—making the Civic Arena the first retractable roof arena constructed in the United States. Ironically, this most notable feature wasn't utilized after 1994 due to several issues with its hydraulic system.

Regardless of its unique exterior, what made the arena so important in the memory of most Pittsburgh sports fans is what happened inside the legendary facility, particularly the exploits of its oldest tenant, the Pittsburgh Penguins.

Former Pittsburgh coach and player Gene Ubriaco said it best when he described the building. "It was beautiful," he said. "I can remember because the roof was round and white and pristine. It was like playing in a cloud. Imagine it's almost like you're playing in the Vatican. It was very unique."[1]

Like the teams that played there, the building itself experienced some ups and downs. From the presence of padlocks outside the Penguin offices in the arena when the team couldn't pay its debts and had to declare bankruptcy in 1975 to championships won by both the Penguins and the American Hockey League Hornets, the arena had been the place where Pittsburgh hockey fans gathered for the better part of five decades.

As the first decade of the twenty-first century rolled by, the Penguins once again began to face financial problems. The key to preventing the franchise from moving was to build a new arena where the team could tap into new revenue resources to both survive and thrive. After months of tense negotiations with the state, an agreement was forged that would see the construction of one of the great new facilities in the NHL, the Consol Energy Center, which would open in October 2010. As the 2009–10 NHL season unfolded, the Civic Arena's days became numbered.

Finally on April 8, 2010, the Pens played the New York Islanders in the regular-season home finale, which also would be the last regularly scheduled contest for the Pittsburgh Penguins in the only home they had ever known.

More than 50 former Penguin players, coaches, and executives were on hand to commemorate the occasion in a pregame ceremony. Pittsburgh coach Dan Bylsma was inspired by meeting such a select group of Penguin legends. "Shaking hands with all those guys, it's a bit surreal to be on that bench and see the last home game, the last regular season game in the building," he said. "Those guys and those memories; it was a special night."[2]

The group would also get to witness the defending Stanley Cup champions put on an offensive show against the Islanders.

It started very quickly as two Penguin defenseman turned into offensive forces. Brooks Orpik gave Pittsburgh a 1–0 lead 23 seconds into the contest, and then Alex Goligoski netted a power-play goal just over four minutes later to put the Pens up by two.

After the Isles cut the lead in half with a power-play goal of their own, Evgeni Malkin, who had missed six of the previous seven games with a bruised foot, broke in on New York goaltender Martin Biron, sliding the puck past him to make it 3–1.

The first-period fireworks continued two minutes later when New York narrowed the lead, and then Sidney Crosby closed out the opening session with his 49th goal of the season with a wrist shot from the right side, making the score 4–2 and sending Biron to the bench in favor of Dwayne Roloson.

New York once again made it a one-goal game early in the second period before Pittsburgh turned this back-and-forth game into a rout. Crosby thought he had scored his 50th goal of the season with 5:26 left in the period, but the goal was later credited to veteran Bill Guerin when replays showed that Crosby's slap shot bounced off him. The score that gave Pittsburgh a 5–3 lead was historic nonetheless. The assist that Crosby garnered on the play was the 500th point of his relatively brief career. He became the third-youngest player in NHL history to break the 500-point plateau, behind only Wayne Gretzky and the Penguins' own Mario Lemieux.

Two minutes later, Tyler Kennedy all but put the game away with his 13th goal of the season, further energizing the standing-room-only crowd of 17,132, which saw the home team take its 6–3 advantage into the final period.

Guerin ended the scoring early in the third with his second goal of the game, giving Pittsburgh its final regular-season goal at the Igloo and wrapping up a 7–3 victory.

The Pens would play seven more games at the Mellon Arena in the Stanley Cup playoffs, the last of which was a 5–2 loss to the Montreal Canadiens in Game Seven of the conference semifinals. But for most Penguin fans, it was the regular-season finale that's remembered as a celebration of just how special the team's original home was.

BOX SCORE

Teams	1	2	3	F
New York	2	1	0	3
Pittsburgh	4	2	1	7

Per	Team	Goal (Assist)	Time
1	Pittsburgh	Orpik 2 (Kennedy, Cooke)	:23
1	Pittsburgh	Goligoski 8 (Crosby, Gonchar)	5:01
1	New York	Moulson 28 (Streit, Tavares)	8:29
1	Pittsburgh	Malkin 26	15:15
1	New York	Okposo 18 (Tambellini, Meyer)	17:08
1	Pittsburgh	Crosby 49 (Dupuis, Guerin)	19:02
2	New York	Bailey 16 (Streit, MacDonald)	2:38
2	Pittsburgh	Guerin 20 (Gonchar, Crosby)	14:34
2	Pittsburgh	Kennedy 13 (Staal, Eaton)	16:41
3	Pittsburgh	Guerin 21 (Dupuis, Crosby)	1:46

Team	Goalie	Saves	Goals
New York	Biron	6	4
New York	Roloson	22	3
Pittsburgh	Fleury	32	3

Shots	1	2	3	F
New York	13	14	8	35
Pittsburgh	10	14	11	35

#30

PENGUINS 5, PHILADELPHIA FLYERS 3
APRIL 25, 2009

Shhhhh

Most valuable players and tide-turning moments don't always show up in the box score. There are aspects of sports that statistics don't cover that can sometimes be the difference between winning and losing. When the Pittsburgh Penguins and the Philadelphia Flyers met in the first round of the 2009 playoffs, it was that kind of quiet detail that saved the Penguins just when victory seemed to be slipping away.

Coming off a loss to the Detroit Red Wings in the 2008 Stanley Cup Finals, Pittsburgh was focused on taking the next step and lifting the trophy for the first time in 18 years. After finishing second in the Atlantic Division with 99 points, the Pens faced off against their cross-state rivals hoping to take the first step to their ultimate goal.

Pittsburgh controlled the action early on in the series, capturing the first two contests at the Mellon Arena, the second a 3–2 overtime victory. They lost Game Three but rebounded with a 3–1 win in the fourth game, which gave the Pens a dominant three-games-to-one lead as the two clubs headed back to the Igloo with a chance for Pittsburgh to win the series on its home ice.

Philadelphia halted Pittsburgh's premature plans for the conference semifinals, scoring a shutout victory that shifted the momentum. Game Six would be played in Philadelphia, and with the way the contest started out, it appeared the Flyers were in the driver's seat.

The game was closely fought for most of the opening period, but with under three minutes left Mike Knuble gave the Flyers a 1–0 lead with a goal after a Philly steal. Fifty-one seconds later, Philadelphia's Joffrey Lupul made it a two-goal advantage as the Flyers stretched their streak to five unanswered goals against the Pens over the previous two games.

If things were looking gloomy for Pittsburgh, they looked downright dismal early in the second period. With Sidney Crosby in the penalty box for slashing, Philadelphia's Danny Briere scored his first goal of the series to make it 3–0. Things could have been even worse for Pittsburgh had another open shot by Philadelphia's Claude Giroux not hit the crossbar, narrowly preventing a four-goal deficit.

Just when it appeared the Pens were about to be blown out, their unassuming hero came to the rescue. Looking to give the team a spark, Pittsburgh's Max Talbot challenged Philadelphia tough guy Daniel Carcillo to a fight. Giving almost 20 pounds to his opponent, Talbot was like a sacrificial lamb, and indeed, Carcillo landed two hard rights to send Talbot to the ice. While the Flyer players and fans were cheering wildly, Talbot got up, looked into the crowd, and put his index finger to his lips—the unspoken symbol for silence. Along with the fight, his cocksure gesture was just the inspiration his team needed.

Afterward, Talbot was asked if he thought going after a player he knew he couldn't beat would pick up his team. "I think it was the right time," he said. "The crowd was into it. Sometimes it's gonna work. Sometimes you lose momentum. This time it gave us a little bit of momentum."[1]

That was an understatement. Talbot's show of daring just might have saved their quest for the Stanley Cup.

The results were immediate. Seconds later, Ruslan Fedotenko scored his first playoff goal in five years to make it 3–1, and less than two minutes after that, Pittsburgh defenseman Mark Eaton tipped in a rebound of a shot from Tyler Kennedy to cut the lead to a single goal.

What had been a comfortable Flyer lead suddenly evaporated when Bill Guerin rifled a slap shot at Philadelphia goaltender Martin Biron. Biron stopped it but couldn't hold onto the puck as Crosby skated in to snatch the rebound and direct it into the net to tie the game at three.

As the teams entered the ice for the final period, any hopes that the Flyers could recapture the momentum quickly went away as Pittsburgh defenseman Sergei Gonchar ripped a slap shot that beat Biron 2:19 into the third to give Pittsburgh a lead it would not relinquish.

The Penguin defense then took over and completely stifled the Philadelphia attack, holding the Flyers to just five shots in the third period. Crosby finished off the Pens' cross-state rivals with less than 30 seconds left with an empty-net goal to put the final touches on a 5–3 series-ending victory.

Crosby finished the game with two goals while Fedotenko and Malkin had two points apiece, and Fleury stopped 22 shots. But as impressive as each of those statistics was in the win, it was a single act of toughness and defiance in a fight that Max Talbot had no chance of winning that won this game.

BOX SCORE

Teams	1	2	3	F
Pittsburgh	0	3	2	5
Philadelphia	2	1	0	3

Per	Team	Goal (Assist)	Time
1	Philadelphia	Knuble 2 (Richards)	17:48
1	Philadelphia	Lupel 1 (Giroux, Briere)	18:39
2	Philadelphia	Briere 1 (Gagne, Timonen)	4:06
2	Pittsburgh	Fedotenko 1 (Malkin)	4:35
2	Pittsburgh	Eaton 2 (Kennedy, Fedotenko)	6:32
2	Pittsburgh	Crosby 3 (Guerin, Letang)	16:59
3	Pittsburgh	Gonchar 1 (Malkin, Orpik)	2:19
3	Pittsburgh	Crosby 4	19:32

Team	Goalie	Saves	Goals
Pittsburgh	Fleury	22	3
Philadelphia	Biron	30	4

Shots	1	2	3	F
Pittsburgh	7	20	8	35
Philadelphia	11	9	5	25

BOSTON BRUINS 4, PENGUINS 3
OCTOBER 11, 1984

First Game, First Shift

Pinpointing the exact moment a sports franchise's fortunes change is intriguing and yet very rare. For the Pittsburgh Penguins' championship run in the 1990s, that moment is defined and even calculated down to the precise second: the 2:59 mark of the first period of the opening game of the 1984 season against the Boston Bruins. That was the moment in which their first-round draft pick, on his first NHL shift, took the first shot of what would be a Hall of Fame career, beating Bruin goalie Pete Peeters to give Pittsburgh a 1–0 lead. In that moment, all of the lofty possibilities attached to the young star seemed realistic for a franchise that had previously only been known for losing and financial catastrophes. After all of that, Mario Lemieux was now here to lead them into the future.

As disappointing as the first two-and-a-half decades of their existence had been, the Penguins' previous two campaigns before Lemieux's arrival were the worst. After finishing 31–36–13 in 1982 and almost upsetting the eventual Stanley Cup champion New York Islanders in the first round of the playoffs, the Penguins quickly fell to the bottom of the league in 1982–83. They sputtered defensively, surrendering a whopping 394 goals while garnering only 45 points.

Head coach Eddie Johnston was replaced by Lou Angotti, who took a bad team and made it even worse. While Pittsburgh did improve slightly defensively, allowing 390 goals in 1983–84, it notched a franchise-low point tally of 38. Mired in last place in the Patrick Division for much of the season with no hope of a playoff berth, the Pens were in a hot race for a title of another kind. By securing the league's worst record, they'd be rewarded with the first overall pick in the draft.

Penguin management started making some questionable moves down the stretch, including sending solid starting goaltender Roberto Romano to the minors and trading one of the few stars they had, former Norris Trophy winner Randy Carlyle. New Jersey Devils president Bob Butera, whose club was also in the running for the top draft pick, accused the Penguins of trying to lose. And indeed, Pittsburgh won just three of its final 21 games, twice losing six straight games.

They eventually finished three points below the Devils in the final standings, giving the Penguins the opportunity to snag one of the greatest prizes in NHL history. Lemieux was a once-in-a-lifetime talent who started his tenure with the Pens in a manner that was not so positive. After following his agent's advice to not don a Pittsburgh jersey for the ceremonial photos after being drafted, Lemieux took the Penguins through a very tense negotiation before finally agreeing to a two-year $700,000 contract. For Johnston, now the club's general manager, it was all worth it. "Mario Lemieux is the best player in the draft," he said, "by a mile."[1]

While there was bad blood between hockey fans in Pittsburgh and their newest star, it all ended before three minutes had elapsed in his first game. New coach Bob Berry put Lemieux on the ice for his first shift 1:41 into the game, and the rookie proceeded to steal a pass from future Hall of Fame defenseman Ray Bourque and then came toward goal on a breakaway against Peeters. Lemieux faked a move that pulled the all-star goaltender out of position, then took his first professional shot on goal. Setting the tone for what was to come, it sailed into the net.

Bourque was dumbfounded after the goal. "I tried to pass the puck between his stick and his skate," the defenseman said. "It hit his skate, and he was just gone."[2]

The rest of the game was anticlimactic for Penguins fans, since no matter what happened next, it couldn't top the thrill of Lemieux's first goal. Pittsburgh took a 2–0 lead at the end of the first period and went up 3–1 after Warren Young scored his second goal of the game early in the second period, thanks to Lemieux's first NHL assist.

Boston scored the final three goals of the game to eke out a 4–3 victory, but it mattered little in the long run. The die had been cast and the Penguins' future was bright.

Following the game, Bourque offered a compliment that, in retrospect, turned out to be a massive understatement when he said that Lemieux was "going to be a big help to that club."[3] A big help, indeed—a little over six years after that opening night in Boston, Lemieux helped hockey fans in Pittsburgh to realize a dream that few thought possible when he arrived: the Pittsburgh Penguins hoisting Lord Stanley's cup.

BOX SCORE

Teams	1	2	3	F
Pittsburgh	2	1	0	3
Boston	0	2	2	4

Per	Team	Goal (Assist)	Time
1	Pittsburgh	Lemieux 1	2:59
1	Pittsburgh	Young 1 (Flockhart, Babych)	13:53
2	Boston	Fergus 1 (Byers, Markwart)	8:13
2	Pittsburgh	Young 2 (Lemieux, Kehoe)	16:49
2	Boston	Linesman 1 (O'Reilly, Bourque)	18:56
3	Boston	O'Connell 1 (Silk, Middleton)	:38
3	Boston	Bourque 1 (Middleton, Silk)	14:28

Team	Goalie	Saves	Goals
Pittsburgh	Herron	32	4
Boston	Peeters	22	3

Shots	1	2	3	F
Pittsburgh	12	5	8	25
Boston	12	14	10	36

PENGUINS 7, DETROIT RED WINGS 4
MARCH 27, 1991

Banners

When you visit the great sports arenas and look up to the rafters, you'll see tributes to the history of the hometown teams in the form of championship banners. In the spring of 1991, if you glanced at the ceiling of the Civic Arena in Pittsburgh you saw no banners of any kind. The Penguins had endured 24 barren, title-less seasons until an evening at Detroit's Joe Louis Arena finally ended that streak.

Ironically, for much of the season, the 1990–91 campaign looked like anything but a championship season. Following what appeared to have been a breakout season in 1988–89, the club finished eight games under .500 the next year, and at the beginning of March 1991, they stood only two games over the break-even point.

The club was 12 points behind the New York Rangers for the division crown with 14 games left in the season, primarily because it had played most of the campaign without superstar Mario Lemieux, who was sidelined after a surgery to remove a herniated disc. But the Pens and their fans were about to learn that to build a championship team, it's just as important to have a talented front office as it is to have good players on the ice, and for the first time in their history, the Penguins had just that in head coach Bob Johnson and general manager Craig Patrick.

Johnson had found a way to keep the ship afloat despite not having Lemieux in the lineup, and on March 4, 1991, Patrick made a trade that forever changed the fortunes of the franchise. He sent John Cullen, Zarley Zalapski, and minor-leaguer Jeff Parker to the Hartford Whalers for future Hall of Famer Ron Francis, along with Ulf Samuelsson, who would become one of the greatest defensemen in team history, and Grant Jennings. Within a month, the arena rafters would be barren no more.

Immediately following the deal, New York spiraled into an eight-game losing streak while the Penguins went on an 8–2–1 run that saw them take a two-point lead into a matchup with the Detroit Red Wings. A victory would give the Penguins a four-point advantage with only two games to play, and since they'd won the season series with the Rangers, they would secure the division crown, their first title of any kind. A loss in Detroit and the title would come down to a game at the Madison Square Garden against New York to close out the campaign.

Having to be forced to win in an arena where they traditionally struggled, the Penguins wanted to take control of the Wings early. Detroit showed no intention of lying down for the Pens, though, as left wing Kevin Miller put a shot past Pittsburgh's backup goaltender Frank Pietrangelo to give Detroit a 1–0 lead six minutes into the game.

In that moment, history suggested that the Penguins would implode and find a way to blow this rare opportunity. But this was a different Pittsburgh team.

Less than a minute after Detroit's opening salvo, Paul Coffey scored a power-play goal to tie the contest. Twelve seconds later, rookie Jaromir Jagr scored his 25th of the season to give the Pens their first lead of the day. Then with time running out in the opening period, Bryan Trottier—a veteran of four Stanley Cup championships with the New York Islanders—gave Pittsburgh a two-goal lead. With the way the team had responded after giving up the first score, it looked like the Penguins' first title was only 40 minutes away.

Detroit was determined to hold off the celebration as goals by Doug Crossman and Paul Ysebaert tied the game in the second period. Once again facing adversity, this Pens team demonstrated its determination. Left wing Kevin Stevens once again put Pittsburgh on top, tipping in a slap shot by Coffey to make it 4–3 with only 32 seconds left in the period, and this time, the Penguins would not give the Red Wings the opportunity to answer back.

In the first three minutes of the third, Francis and Jagr each scored, only 34 seconds apart, to increase the advantage to three, and right winger Scott Young put the icing on the cake with his 17th goal of the year midway in the third to make the score 7–3. Detroit's Shawn Burr tallied a meaningless goal with five minutes left, but Pittsburgh accomplished its 24-year-old mission. Veterans like Phil Bourque, who had suffered for so long to get to this point, could truly enjoy the moment.

"I remember in my second or third year when we had 5,000 people in the building and we were losing all the time," he said. "I'd go home and people would say, 'Bourque, you've got to get out of that organization.' I told them 'no way' because I knew our time would come."[1]

On this night, their time finally had come. And within the next two months, Pittsburgh would acquire two more banners by capturing their first conference title and Stanley Cup championship, ensuring that the Civic Arena ceiling would be bare no more.

BOX SCORE

Teams	1	2	3	F
Pittsburgh	3	1	3	7
Detroit	1	2	1	4

Per	Team	Goal (Assist)	Time
1	Detroit	Miller 20 (Burr, Racine)	6:18
1	Pittsburgh	Coffey 23 (Stevens, Recchi)	7:03
1	Pittsburgh	Jagr 25 (Roberts, Recchi)	7:15
1	Pittsburgh	Trottier 9 (Gilhen, Loney)	19:12
2	Detroit	Crossman 8 (Federov, Fedyk)	1:52
2	Detroit	Ysebaert 17 (Probert)	12:25
2	Pittsburgh	Stevens 39 (Coffey, Recchi)	19:28
3	Pittsburgh	Francis 23 (Stevens, Samuelsson)	1:57
3	Pittsburgh	Jagr 26 (Jennings, Loney)	2:31
3	Pittsburgh	S. Young 17 (Jennings)	8:53
3	Detroit	Burr 20 (Racine, Yzerman)	14:52

Team	Goalie	Saves	Goals
Pittsburgh	Pietrangelo	28	4
Detroit	Cheveldae	16	7
Detroit	Hanlon	3	0

Shots	1	2	3	F
Pittsburgh	9	8	9	26
Detroit	12	11	9	32

#27

PENGUINS 4, NEW JERSEY DEVILS 3
APRIL 22, 1993

Where No Team Has Gone Before

Any discussion of Pittsburgh Penguins winning streaks begins and ends with their historic 17-game string during the 1992–93 season, which broke the NHL record. As incredible as that streak was, there is another that gets less attention but might be even more impressive.

When the Pittsburgh Penguins met the New Jersey Devils in Game Three of the first round of the 1993 playoffs, the Pens had a chance to capture their 14th consecutive postseason victory—which would break the NHL record of 13 set by the Edmonton Oilers in 1985 and would signify a downright astonishing achievement.

To put it in perspective across the sports spectrum, the National Football League record was 10, set by the New England Patriots during their triumphant run in the early 2000s, and the New York Yankees held the Major League Baseball mark with 12, strung together between 1927 and 1932. And the Los Angeles Lakers held the historical distinction in the National Basketball Association, capturing 13 consecutive postseason victories in a two-year period between 1988 and 1989. A win against the Devils and the Penguins would have gone where no team in North American major professional sports had before.

It had already been a magnificent season for the Pittsburgh Penguins. Coming off back-to-back Stanley Cup championships, they not only eclipsed the league record for consecutive victories but set the franchise marks for victories in a season (56) and points (119) while capturing their only President Cup trophy, awarded to the best team in the league for the regular season.

They began their defense of the Stanley Cup with two easy wins over New Jersey in the Patrick Division semifinals to give them a comfortable lead in the series and tie the league's eight-year-old record for consecutive postseason wins.

Amazingly, Pittsburgh's two historic winning streaks dovetailed. The Pens had carried their 17-game winning streak right up to the regular-season finale, which they tied, and then picked up where they left off by extending their postseason string. Going into Game Three against the Devils, the Penguins hadn't lost a game in nearly seven weeks.

For as easy as the first two games of the series had been for Pittsburgh, New Jersey wasn't going to allow the Pens to set the all-time major professional sports record without a fight.

New Jersey's Bill Guerin—who would one day play for another Pittsburgh Stanley Cup winner—opened the scoring one minute into the game after intercepting a pass from Pens defenseman Ulf Samuelsson and putting a shot past Pittsburgh goalie Tom Barrasso. It would be the only goal Barrasso gave up in the first period, as he kept the Pens in the contest by stopping 15 of the 16 shots New Jersey rifled at him. Barrasso's opening-period heroics allowed the Penguins to keep the game close; then Shawn McEachern tied it midway through the period, scoring after a great pass by Martin Straka for his third goal of the series.

While the game was tied, the New Jersey defense was suffocating the high-scoring Penguin attack in the first period, allowing only seven shots on goal, including three meaningless shots when Pittsburgh had a five-minute man advantage. The Pens picked things up in the second period with 16 shots, but it was Devils goalie Craig Billington's turn to shine as he turned away each one. With the Pittsburgh offense stonewalled, New Jersey took the lead at the 16:42 mark of the second period when Bobby Holik scored to make it 2–1, Devils.

Going into the third period, the Penguins were in uncharted waters. They'd grown accustomed to leading at this point in the game, and held a record of just 2–13–1 over the course of the season when trailing after two periods. Pittsburgh coach Scotty Bowman had confidence his team could battle back though, despite being outplayed for most of the game. "That gave us a lot of hope we could win this game," he said.[1]

With their date with history now in jeopardy, the Pens quickly fought back. Clutch goals are usually scored by clutch players, and for the Penguins, Mario Lemieux came through in those situations. Only a minute into the third, Lemieux ripped a shot from just inside the face-off circle past Billington to once again tie the score.

While one of the greatest scorers in NHL history tied the game up, it would be one of the least prodigious scorers on the ice who put the Pens ahead. In 451 games during his 11-year NHL career, defenseman Peter Taglianetti had scored a mere 18 goals and would score only two in 53 career playoff games.

Luckily for the Penguins, one of the two put them ahead for good. Taglianetti found lady luck on his side when his slap shot bounced off Devil center Alexander Semak and flew past Billington to give Pittsburgh a 3–2 lead. With the momentum shifted, just over two minutes later, Larry Murphy increased the Penguins' lead to two goals with a power-play tally after taking a pass from Rick Tocchet.

As Pittsburgh was only 10 minutes away from history, New Jersey refused to go down quietly. Semak cut the margin to one 13 seconds later, but the Pittsburgh defense held New Jersey to just five shots in the final period to close out the victory and secure the Penguins' place in the record books.

While they finally lost in the next contest to the Devils before closing out the series, the Penguins' incredible mark still stands more than two decades later—tops among every major sports league in North America.

BOX SCORE

Teams	1	2	3	F
Pittsburgh	1	0	3	4
New Jersey	1	1	1	3

Per	Team	Goal (Assist)	Time
1	New Jersey	Guerin 1	1:03
1	Pittsburgh	McEachern 3 (Straka)	9:36
2	New Jersey	Holik 1 (S. Stevens)	16:32
3	Pittsburgh	M. Lemieux 4 (Murphy, Ramsey)	1:07
3	Pittsburgh	Taglianetti 1 (Loney, Tippett)	7:05
3	Pittsburgh	Murphy 1 (Francis, Tocchet)	9:31
3	New Jersey	Semak 1 (Zelepukin)	9:44

Team	Goalie	Saves	Goals
Pittsburgh	Barrasso	29	3
New Jersey	Billington	31	4

Shots	1	2	3	F
Pittsburgh	7	16	12	35
New Jersey	16	11	5	32

#26

Two Minutes to Remember

An old sports axiom states that a team must go all out for an entire game in order to win—and not just coast to victory playing well only in the final minutes. While there have certainly been occasions in which a team hasn't played particularly well down the stretch and still managed to hang on for the win, the St. Louis Blues became the exception to the old cliché in a dramatic fashion when they met the Pittsburgh Penguins at the Civic Arena on a cold November evening in 1972.

After playing hard for nearly three quarters of the contest, the Blues witnessed a scoring burst—unseen in the annals of the National Hockey League—that quickly turned a tight game into a blowout. For the Penguins, it was truly two minutes to remember.

Both Pittsburgh and St. Louis entered the NHL in 1967 and, for the better part of the first five years of their existence, went in opposite directions. St. Louis contended for Stanley Cup championships while the Pens were mired in the bottom half of their division. By 1972, led by a strong core of young players such as Syl Apps, Al McDonough, and Jean Pronovost, Pittsburgh had evened the playing field.

They had defeated the Blues 5–2 in their first meeting of the season and came into their second matchup game riding a three-game winning streak. They stood at 10–9–1 while St. Louis had struggled to a 4–8–5 mark.

Pittsburgh started off the game on a high note. After the Blues' 40-goal scorer Gary Unger was sent off the ice first for slashing, then strongly disagreed with the call and received a 10-minute misconduct infraction, Apps scored a power-play goal, tipping in a slap shot by defenseman Jack Lynch to give the Pens a 1–0 lead.

Eight minutes later, Pittsburgh's Brian "Bugsy" Watson did something he

97

only accomplished 17 times in his 17-year career when he tallied his only goal of the 1972–73 campaign with a slap shot from the right point to put Pittsburgh up by two.

After St. Louis right wing Phil Roberto cut the lead to one, the Penguins quickly restored their two-goal advantage when Apps hit McDonough with a perfect pass and McDonough stuffed it past St. Louis goalie Wayne Stephenson for the 3–1 lead, which endured through the end of the first period.

The Blues fought back to tie the score in the second and then took the lead just over a minute into the third. At that point the Blues were completely dominating the game and appeared on their way to a comeback victory—unaware that the lead they had worked so hard to achieve was about to be erased in a spectacular manner.

Thirty-four seconds later, McDonough scored his second goal of the game to tie the contest at four. Greg Polis then regained the lead for Pittsburgh with a little over 10 minutes left. Fifty-two minutes were in the book, and it was still a closely fought game.

Then the record-setting two-minute surge began.

Bryan Hextall started the onslaught when he tipped in another Lynch slap shot with exactly eight minutes left to give the Pens a 6–4 lead. Twelve seconds later Pronovost netted his fifth of the year before McDonough completed his hat trick at the 13:40 mark to increase the advantage to four.

In case three goals in 100 seconds wasn't impressive enough, future Penguin coach Ken Schinkel took it to the next level, gathering a pass from Ron Schock to score only nine seconds later to make it 9–4. Schock finished the assault with 5:53 left when he scored the Penguins' 10th goal.

When the dust had settled, the feat proved remarkable. Despite being outshot 42–34, the Penguins had notched a comfortable victory with the final five scores coming in an astonishing two minutes and seven seconds—setting an NHL record that hasn't come close to being broken. In fact when bleacherreport. com compiled a list of the 33 most unbreakable NHL records in December of 2011, the Penguins' scoring show from November 1972 was on the list.

For two periods, it didn't feel like a memorable evening, but those two minutes and seven seconds will never be forgotten.

BOX SCORE

Teams	1	2	3	F
St. Louis	1	2	1	4
Pittsburgh	3	0	7	10

Per	Team	Goal (Assist)	Time
1	Pittsburgh	Apps 9 (Lynch, McDonough)	3:59
1	Pittsburgh	Watson 1 (Edestrand, Kessell)	11:40
1	St. Louis	Roberto 3 (Murphy)	13:50
1	Pittsburgh	McDonough 9 (Apps)	14:31
2	St. Louis	Roberto 4 (Huck, Thomson)	1:58
2	St. Louis	O'Shea 3 (Evans)	7:36
3	St. Louis	Huck 3 (Roberto, Murphy)	1:22
3	Pittsburgh	McDonough 10 (Apps)	1:56
3	Pittsburgh	Polis (Pronovost, Hextall)	9:05
3	Pittsburgh	Hextall 9 (Lynch, Polis)	12:00
3	Pittsburgh	Pronovost 5 (Polis)	12:18
3	Pittsburgh	McDonough 11 (Apps)	13:40
3	Pittsburgh	Schinkel 10 (Burrows, Schock)	13:49
3	Pittsburgh	Schock (Schinkel, Lynch)	14:07

Team	Goalie	Saves	Goals
St. Louis	Stephenson	24	10
Pittsburgh	Rutherford	38	4

Shots	1	2	3	F
St. Louis	13	15	14	42
Pittsburgh	10	9	15	34

#25

PENGUINS 6, PHILADELPHIA FLYERS 0
MAY 18, 2008

The Keystone Champions

The Keystone State rivalry between Pennsylvania's two biggest cities has been legendary and often bitter. Naturally, sports have been a big part of it: Eagles vs. Steelers, Pirates vs. Phillies, and it's even spilled over into college basketball with the University of Pittsburgh and Villanova University. But among all the sports, there has been one rivalry that has been more bitterly contested than the others, that of the Philadelphia Flyers and the Pittsburgh Penguins.

Going into the 2007–08 season, the interesting thing about the rivalry is that despite the fact the Penguins and Flyers had each won two Stanley Cups apiece, it had been a very one-sided affair, with Philadelphia holding a decisive 124–76–31 advantage. The Flyers' dominance had also carried over to the postseason, as they won all three series between the teams. The Penguins hoped to change the trend when the teams met in the 2008 Eastern Conference Finals.

Led by Sidney Crosby, Evgeni Malkin, and Marc-Andre Fleury, the Penguins may have had the edge, having garnered more points in winning the Atlantic Division crown. But as usual, the Flyers had won the season series, and with a trip to the Stanley Cup Finals on the line, history seemed to dictate that somehow Philadelphia would emerge victorious once again.

The Flyers' optimism withered when the Pens took a three-games-to-one advantage in the series. But even this comfortable lead wasn't enough to quiet the ghosts of the past. It stirred echoes of 1989, when the Penguins were just a victory away from knocking off Philly in the division finals but lost two straight to end their season. So even as dominant as Pittsburgh had looked through the first four games, 19 years later, most Penguin fans still braced for the worst.

Crosby and Malkin helped ease their fears early on. Physical right winger Ryan Malone, the son of former Penguin Greg Malone, scored a power-play goal off a perfect pass from Crosby to give the Pens an early 1–0 lead. Seven minutes later Malone made a spectacular play, stealing the puck from goalie Martin Biron from behind the net and then feeding it to Malkin, who stuffed it into the net to increase the lead to two.

As impressive as the Penguins were in the first period, things only got better in the second. High-scoring right winger Marian Hossa, whom general manager Ray Shero had picked up from the Atlanta Thrashers in a trade-deadline deal, scored his ninth goal of the playoffs 8:24 into the period to make it 3–0. And three minutes later, Malone netted his second power-play goal of the contest off a pass from Hossa to put Pittsburgh in front by four.

While long-time Penguin fans could still envision the Flyers scoring four quick goals to get back into it, Pittsburgh's third-line center, Jordan Staal, scored another goal with only 58 seconds left in the second to make it 5–0.

Whatever fears remained now evaporated. Chants of "Let's go, Pens!" and "Go home, Flyers!" echoed through the Civic Arena.

Four minutes into the final period, Pascal Dupuis, the second piece of the Hossa trade, put the icing on the cake when he pulled in a pass from his former Atlanta teammate to round out the scoring.

The Pittsburgh defense held firm the rest of the way, helping Fleury notch a shutout as the Pens completed their worst-to-first turnaround by celebrating their first Eastern Conference crown. The youthful Penguins were thrilled. "It's unbelievable just to realize we're four wins away," Pittsburgh defenseman Ryan Whitney said after the contest. "It hasn't really sunk in yet that these next few games are the Stanley Cup Finals."[1]

When Crosby went to center ice to receive the Eastern Conference trophy, he refused to touch it—in keeping with the NHL tradition of not wanting to hoist a trophy before a team wins the Stanley Cup. "We all realized it's not the one we want to be holding," Crosby stated. "We want the big trophy," Hossa added.[2]

While holding the Stanley Cup was the ultimate prize, making the conference crown a little more meaningful was the unofficial title that went with it: Keystone State champions.

BOX SCORE

Teams	1	2	3	F
Philadelphia	0	0	0	0
Pittsburgh	2	3	1	6

Per	Team	Goal (Assist)	Time
1	Pittsburgh	Malone 5 (Crosby, Hossa)	2:30
1	Pittsburgh	Malkin 9 (Malone)	9:50
2	Pittsburgh	Hossa 9 (Crosby, Talbot)	8:24
2	Pittsburgh	Malone 6 (Gonchar, Hossa)	11:42
2	Pittsburgh	Staal 6 (Talbot, Hall)	19:02
3	Pittsburgh	Dupuis 2 (Hossa, Orpik)	4:03

Team	Goalie	Saves	Goals
Philadelphia	Biron	19	6
Pittsburgh	Fleury	21	0

Shots	1	2	3	F
Philadelphia	5	8	8	21
Pittsburgh	10	9	6	25

PENGUINS 4, DETROIT RED WINGS 3

JUNE 2, 2008

Put Stanley Back in the Case

While there are many cherished trophies in sports, none has quite the history of the Stanley Cup. Its traditions are numerous. The oldest demands that the winners drink champagne from the trophy and that the team captain is the first to hoist it after it is awarded. Another tradition states that the winning team gets the trophy for 100 days after the title is won so it can be passed around among the players and front office personnel so each person can spend a day or two with it before it's sent back to be displayed at the Hall of Fame.

Perhaps the most interesting tradition occurs on the night it could potentially be awarded. When a team is one win away from capturing the NHL championship, the cup is brought into the arena in a black case protected by two guards with white gloves. The revered trophy is taken out of the case, polished, and readied for the NHL commissioner to award it to the victorious team. Both encouraging and intimidating, it's a practice that can be used to explain the psychology behind both clutch performances and heartbreaking failures.

A perfect example occurred on June 2, 2008, when the Pittsburgh Penguins and Detroit Red Wings stepped on to the ice at Detroit's Joe Louis Arena with the Red Wings enjoying a commanding three-games-to-one advantage. While the Stanley Cup guards were busy preparing it for a Red Wing victory, the Pens entered the game with a clear mission: to force them to put Stanley back in the case.

While Detroit's lead in the series was comfortable, the previous two games in the series had been hard fought, with Pittsburgh emerging victorious in Game Three, 3–2, before blowing a 1–0 first-period lead in a 2–1 loss to the Red Wings in Game Four. Though they were a defeat away from elimination, the Pens at least had proved they were competitive with Detroit and were confident they could keep the cup from appearing on this evening.

Pittsburgh started off strong in the first period, forging a quick lead when Marian Hossa netted his 11th goal of the postseason after taking a perfect pass from Pascal Dupuis and sending it past Detroit goaltender Chris Osgood for a 1–0 lead.

Three minutes later, Pittsburgh right wing Adam Hall, who'd scored only two goals in the regular season, tallied his third in the Stanley Cup playoffs—though it was actually more of a gift from Detroit, as it was technically put into the net by a Wings defenseman. Regardless of who deserved the credit, Pittsburgh carried a surprising 2–0 lead into the second period.

Like in the previous game, the Red Wings' defense toughened up after Pittsburgh opened up an early lead, which enabled the Detroit offense to spark a comeback. The resurgence began when center Darren Helm rifled a shot past Pens netminder Marc-Andre Fleury to cut the lead in half at the 2:54 mark of the second period. But the Penguin defense was able to hold on the rest of the period, and Pittsburgh clung to its 2–1 lead into the third period, where the home team's fortunes would quickly reverse.

Pittsburgh's Tyler Kennedy was sent to the penalty box for hooking six minutes into the third, and Detroit wasted little time in taking advantage when Pavel Datsyuk tied the game with the Red Wings' first power-play goal of the evening. Pens coach Michel Therrien called a time out, hoping to calm his young team down, to no avail. The Red Wings took the lead just over a minute later when Johan Franzen found defenseman Brian Rafalski with a pass and Rafalski ripped a shot past the Pens' goalie. With a 3–2 lead, the Red Wings were suddenly only 10 minutes and 37 seconds away from hoisting Lord Stanley's cup.

With the support of the sellout crowd behind them and their ample playoff experience, the Red Wings were, by all appearances, on the brink of another championship. As time was winding down and the celebration became imminent, Therrien pulled Fleury and sent Max Talbot onto the ice in a desperate attempt to tie the game. With less than 40 seconds remaining, Hossa took the puck from behind the net and directed a shot toward Osgood that bounced off his pads. Then Talbot destroyed the Red Wings' plans when he skated toward the net and directed the puck past the Detroit goalie to tie the score at the 19:25 mark. The fans, counting down the seconds to a championship, were stunned into silence. With the game now even, the two teams were about to begin one of the most memorable overtime sessions in the history of the Stanley Cup Finals. One that took three extra periods to conclude.

The Penguins had the best opportunity to score in the first two overtimes—with Evgeni Malkin ripping a shot off the arm of Osgood before Osgood finally grabbed it—but the Red Wings thoroughly dominated play. They outshot the Pens 13–2 in the first overtime, while Fleury prevented elimination by stopping all 20 Red Wing shots in the first two extra frames.

The Penguins caught a break at the 9:21 mark of the third overtime when Detroit center Jiri Hudler's stick hit Pens defenseman Rob Scuderi in the face. The high stick drew blood, causing a four-minute double minor penalty on Detroit for a Pittsburgh power play. "I was just praying for blood," the Pens defenseman said later.[1]

The stage was set for right winger Petr Sykora, who was in this position once before. In 2003, he'd ended the fourth-longest game in the history of the Stanley Cup Finals when he scored an overtime goal for the triumphant Anaheim Ducks. Just after the Detroit penalty was called, Sykora promptly ended the fifth-longest game in finals history when he rifled a shot past Osgood to end the contest at 12:36 a.m., four and a half hours after it had begun.

In a contest defined by second chances, it was only fitting that Sykora had ended it by giving his team new life. "We have a great thing going right now," he said. "We just wanted to win this game. We didn't really look ahead. Now we're going back home. We've got nothing to lose. We know what we have to do, and hopefully we can bring it back here to Detroit."[2]

While the Penguins' magic ran out in a narrow 2–1 loss in Game Six, on this night in hostile territory they'd done what was needed to keep their season alive.

And keep the Stanley Cup boxed up for another day.

BOX SCORE

Teams	1	2	3	OT	OT	OT	F
Pittsburgh	2	0	1	0	0	1	4
Detroit	0	1	2	0	0	0	3

Per	Team	Goal (Assist)	Time
1	Pittsburgh	Hossa 11 (Crosby, Dupuis)	8:37
1	Pittsburgh	Hall 3	14:41
2	Detroit	Helm 2 (Maltby)	2:54
3	Detroit	Datsyuk 10 (Zetterberg, Rafalski)	6:43
3	Detroit	Rafalski 3 (Franzen, Zetterberg)	9:23
3	Pittsburgh	Talbot 3 (Hossa, Crosby)	19:25
3OT	Pittsburgh	Sykora 6 (Malkin, Gonchar)	9:57

Team	Goalie	Saves	Goals
Pittsburgh	Fleury	55	3
Detroit	Osgood	28	4

Shots	1	2	3	OT	OT	OT	F
Pittsburgh	7	7	4	2	8	4	32
Detroit	8	12	14	13	7	4	58

PENGUINS 2, BUFFALO SABRES 1
JANUARY 1, 2008

The Great Outdoors

Until the twenty-first century, outdoor hockey in North America was primarily only for the children of Canada, playing on their makeshift backyard rinks, ponds, and lakes. As the first decade of the new century began, playing outdoors went from a tradition reserved for children to one that included the best hockey players in the world. And as a result, hockey teams were suddenly playing in large outdoor stadiums in front of massive crowds that would have been thought to be unimaginable only a few years before.

Spurred by the success of outdoor collegiate hockey games in East Lansing, Michigan, and Madison, Wisconsin, as well as a contest at Edmonton in 2003, where the Oilers hosted the Montreal Canadiens in front of a chilled 57,167 fans who endured sub-zero temperatures, NBC sports executive John Miller decided to present the concept of an annual outdoor game to the NHL in 2004. Initially unable to forge an agreement with the league, Miller sold the idea to another NBC sports executive who helped him finally convince the NHL that his concept was sound.

And the Winter Classic was born.

The league and NBC chose New Year's Day for what would become the marquee event of the NHL's regular season. The setting for the inaugural contest would be Ralph Wilson Stadium in Buffalo, where the Sabres played host to a young Pittsburgh Penguin team.

Though the Pens were only 19–16–2 coming into this contest, the league wanted to showcase the teams' two young stars, Sidney Crosby and Evgeni Malkin. After failing to make the playoffs for four straight years, the Pens turned in a surprising 105-point campaign in 2006–07 with Crosby and Malkin leading the way. The NHL was banking that Pittsburgh would become a perennial contender for the Stanley Cup.

The Penguins had struggled to pick up where they'd left off to start the 2007–8 campaign, but after a 4–2 loss to the New York Islanders on December 21, they'd won three consecutive games to close out the calendar year. To continue the momentum, Pittsburgh would have to contend with not only an NHL record 71,217 patrons but something that made this game so intriguing: the elements.

Winter in Buffalo is not for the faint of heart, and this New Year's Day would be no different: a cold, blustery day with high winds and snow that increased with ferocity as the game went on. The conditions may not have been conducive to flawless hockey, but for those who experienced playing the game as children in the great north, they were perfect.

With the elements a factor throughout the game, Penguins right winger Colby Armstrong gave Pittsburgh a quick lead before the snow increased its intensity, scoring 21 seconds into the game to make it 1–0 before the fans could settle into their seats.

After the quick goal, Penguin goaltender Ty Conklin and Buffalo's Ryan Miller settled down. Except for a goal by the Sabres' Brian Campbell 1:25 into the second period, both goalies became proverbial brick walls in front of their respective cages. Maintenance crews tried to keep the ice as clean as possible— using the Zamboni in the middle of each period as well as in between—but as regulation was quickly coming to an end, the attempts proved to be impossible.

The snow became much heavier with five minutes left in regulation and continued as the teams battled into overtime. Buffalo dominated the extra session, outshooting the Penguins 7–0, as the contest resembled the tone of the second period, when the Sabres held a 14–2 shot advantage. But for as much pressure as the Sabres put on Conklin, the Pens' goalie kept Pittsburgh in the game.

Through the steadily falling snow, the five-minute overtime period came to an end with the game still knotted at one goal apiece. Miller's dream of an outdoor hockey game had proven more exciting than he could have imagined, and now the two clubs would end the affair with a shootout. The teams decided to go to the west end of the rink to try to avoid the snow as much as possible.

Buffalo continued its overtime momentum as Ales Kotalik began the shootout by beating Conklin with a wrist shot to give the Sabres a 1–0 advantage in the three-shot matchup. After the Penguins' Eric Christensen completely missed the net, Conklin stopped Tim Connolly's attempt. Next up for the Pens was rookie defenseman Kris Letang, who was already three-for-three during shootouts in his young career. True to form, Letang kept the streak alive with a backhander past Miller to tie up the shootout at one score apiece.

The Pens' goalie made another fine save on Buffalo's third shot, a backhand by Maxim Afinogenov. The save gave the NHL and NBC a dream scenario: rising star Sidney Crosby, the new face of the league, as the last scheduled shooter with a chance to win the game.

With the snow falling and the excited fans on their feet, Crosby gave the powers that be exactly what they wanted. He scored the dramatic, game-winning goal and then quickly skated into the waiting arms of his teammates.

The thrilled young superstar loved both the moment and the atmosphere. "Growing up, I played a lot outside," Crosby said, remembering his days in Nova Scotia. "When you see 70,000 people jammed into a stadium to watch hockey, it's a good sign. The atmosphere and environment—I don't think you can beat that."[1]

NBC and the NHL agreed. Thanks to the weather and Crosby's exciting shootout goal, the Winter Classic has become a New Year's Day tradition, an even bigger event than the NHL All-Star Game that follows a few weeks later.

In retrospect, the idea seems natural for most hard-core hockey fans—especially those in the northern climates, where the Winter Classic evokes happy memories of the outdoor games they played as children.

BOX SCORE

Teams	1	2	3	OT	SO	F
Pittsburgh	1	0	0	0	1	2
Buffalo	0	1	0	0	0	1

Per	Team	Goal (Assist)	Time
1	Pittsburgh	Armstrong 6 (Crosby)	:21
2	Buffalo	Campbell 4 (Connolly, Paille)	1:25

Shootout	Goalie	Shooter	Result	Score
Buffalo	Conklin	Kotalik	Goal	0–1
Pittsburgh	Miller	Christensen	Miss	0–1
Buffalo	Conklin	Connolly	Miss	0–1
Pittsburgh	Miller	Letang	Goal	1–1
Buffalo	Conklin	Afinogenov	Miss	1–1
Pittsburgh	Miller	Crosby	Goal	2–1

Team	Goalie	Saves	Goals
Pittsburgh	Conklin	36	1
Buffalo	Miller	24	1

Shots	1	2	3	OT	F
Pittsburgh	11	2	12	0	25
Buffalo	9	14	7	7	37

#22

Mario 2.0

To say that Mario Lemieux had the greatest career of any player in Pittsburgh Penguins history would be a dramatic understatement, but while Lemieux is the unquestioned king of Penguin hockey, his career was cut short.

Lemieux was forced to retire at the age of 31 because of several chronic maladies that paralleled his scoring titles, MVP awards, and championships. Severe back issues, tendonitis in his hip flexor muscle, and even cancer had broken down Lemieux's body over his 12-year career, and following the 1996–97 campaign, during which he captured his sixth scoring title, he decided he'd had enough. Lemieux retired as the only NHL player to end his career with an average of over two points per game, and so impressive was his career that the league waived its normal three-year waiting period and promptly inducted the Pens' superstar into the Hall of Fame.

While he was no longer on the ice, Mario Lemieux stayed very active in the game of hockey, becoming even more important to the franchise that he'd led to their only two Stanley Cup championships. By the end of the twentieth century, the team was in bankruptcy after years of offering aggressively high contracts trying to keep its talented team together. Owners Howard Baldwin and Morris Belzberg were in debt for $90 million, and their biggest creditor was their former captain, Mario Lemieux, to whom they owed $30 million.

Wanting not only to collect his dues but to save the franchise from having to relocate, Lemieux struck a deal to turn the money they owed to him into equity in the team, and he officially took over the franchise as its majority owner on September 1, 1999.

As principal owner, he and general manager Craig Patrick went about trying to find the type of Hall of Fame player to add to their roster in the hopes of competing for another Stanley Cup. But, still mired in the team's financial issues, they had to find one who wouldn't be paid like a superstar. That December, they found their man—Lemieux himself.

Missing the game he once dominated, he felt he could be the final piece to the Pens' championship quest. The news was like an unexpected Christmas present for Penguins fans, and he chose December 27, 2000, for his comeback, in a game against the Toronto Maple Leafs.

A sellout crowd of 17,148 descended on the Civic Arena, and the game was broadcast nationally across the U.S. and Canada. Not surprisingly, the atmosphere was electric. The fans rose to their feet as the arena maintenance crew symbolically took down the banner from the rafters with Lemieux's number emblazoned on it—for while his achievements of the past were still as revered, as of this night, his career wasn't over yet.

Yet for as much excitement and optimism as his return created, there was some doubt about whether a star player could come back to the game at a comparable level after being away for more than three years. It was difficult to imagine Lemieux picking up where he left off. But this was one of the greatest players ever to grace the ice, and he was capable of achieving the seemingly impossible.

Only 33 seconds into the game Lemieux showed that he hadn't lost his incredible playmaking skills, as he fed Jaromir Jagr with a perfect pass that led to a goal to give Pittsburgh a quick 1–0 lead. While it was a special moment, it paled in comparison to what happened midway through the second period. Pittsburgh had already extended its lead to 2–0 when Jagr found Lemieux in the right slot, and Lemieux put a one-timer past Toronto goalie Chris Joseph for his first goal since April 11, 1997.

With the crowd roaring almost in disbelief, time seemed to stand still—much as it seemingly had done for Lemieux. Mario "2.0" seemed just as incredible as the original version who'd arrived in Pittsburgh 16 years earlier. Later, Lemieux added another assist on a goal by Jiri Hrdina, and Jagr netted his second of the game to give Pittsburgh a 5–0 victory.

Even Mario was a little surprised by his performance. "Overall, I think it was a good performance for everybody, and I'm glad it's over," he said. "That's what I had in mind, to play my first game and be successful and to play at a high level. I was a little bit surprised at how I played. My legs were strong."[1]

While the victory was impressive and there were other standouts, this game would be remembered for one reason only: the new version of Mario Lemieux would be just as spectacular as the old.

BOX SCORE

Teams	1	2	3	F
Toronto	0	0	0	0
Pittsburgh	2	3	0	5

Per	Team	Goal (Assist)	Time
1	Pittsburgh	Jagr 20 (Hrdina, Lemieux)	:33
1	Pittsburgh	Kovalev 19 (Straka, Laukkanen)	10:19
2	Pittsburgh	Lemieux 1 (Jagr, Kasparaitis)	10:33
2	Pittsburgh	Hrdina 9 (Lemieux, Jagr)	14:23
2	Pittsburgh	Jagr 21	19:57

Team	Goalie	Saves	Goals
Toronto	Joseph	26	5
Pittsburgh	Snow	40	0

Shots	1	2	3	F
Toronto	5	12	23	40
Pittsburgh	13	12	6	31

On December 20, 1988, Penguins superstar Mario Lemieux broke through two Islander defenders on his way to a spectacular goal. Twenty-four years later his memorable score was immortalized in a statue that stands outside of the Penguins' new home at the Consol Energy Center. (Author's collection)

Until the Pittsburgh Penguins defeated the Detroit Red Wings on March 27, 1991, to win the Patrick Division, the walls at the Civic Arena were barren. Today many banners decorate their new home at the Consol Energy Center, including several that list players who won both scoring titles and MVP awards as a Penguin. (Author's collection)

Electing to sign a professional contract rather than become a member of the famed 1980 Olympic squad, Joe Mullen went on to become one of the greatest American players in the history of the sport. Scoring 502 goals in his career, Mullen spent his last few years in the NHL, mostly with the Pens, scoring 42 goals in 1991–92. (Courtesy of Boston College Athletics)

Coming on the short end of more than their share of games against the Philadelphia Flyers, their cross-state rivals, the Penguins finally got the best of them in 2008, defeating the Flyers in the Eastern Conference Finals. In this contest, number 87, Sidney Crosby, looks to deflect the puck into the Philadelphia net. (Author's collection)

Opened in 1961 as the home of the Pittsburgh Civic Light Opera, the Civic Arena was a marvel as the country's first sports venue with a retractable roof. In 1967 it became the first home of the Pittsburgh Penguins. They remained there for 43 years, playing their final regular season contest against the New York Islanders on April 8, 2010. (Author's collection)

A former second-round pick by Anaheim out of St. Cloud State, Matt Cullen proved to be the effective veteran leader Penguins GM Jim Rutherford had hoped for when he signed the 39-year-old to a free agent contract before the 2015–16 campaign. Cullen netted 16 goals in helping to lead Pittsburgh to their fourth Stanley Cup title. (Courtesy of St. Cloud State University Athletic Media Relations)

Mario Lemieux turned the fortunes of the hapless Pittsburgh Penguins to that of the two-time Stanley Cup championships in 1991 and 1992. A decade later, he once again came to the rescue, this time as owner, helping not only to save them from bankruptcy but to build them to winners again. Pictured above are Lemieux (left) and coowner Ron Burkle (right), riding in the parade after the club captured its third title in 2009. (Photo courtesy of Vivian Finoli)

After starting his collegiate career at Boston College, Ben Lovejoy transferred to Dartmouth where he was not only an outstanding hockey player but an All-Ivy league Lacrosse player. Signed as a free-agent by the Pens, he was an up-and-coming star before being dealt to Anaheim in 2013 where he lived up to his potential. Pittsburgh reacquired him in 2015 as he was a pivotal piece of their Stanley Cup run in 2016. (Courtesy of Dartmouth Athletics)

After years of suffering with an arena that could not provide the franchise with the financial output for the team to succeed, the Penguins finally entered the twenty-first century when they opened the Consol Energy Center. The ground breaking was held on August 14, 2008, and was finished almost two years to the day on August 1, 2010. (Author's collection)

In one of the greatest trades in franchise history, the Penguins acquired the first pick in the 2003 NHL entry draft, which they used to acquire the first piece of their second winning era in goaltender Marc-Andre Fleury. Fleury has been the team's most successful goalie, winning a team record 310 games as of January 2015. (Author's collection)

Every team needs a physical presence in front of the net, and for the Pittsburgh Penguins in the first decade of the twenty-first century they had that in Ryan Malone. Malone, about to tip in the puck for a goal against Philadelphia in the photo above, scored 87 goals for Pittsburgh in four seasons as a Penguin between 2003 and 2008. (Author's collection)

Mario Lemieux had his Jaromir Jagr when it came to leading the Pittsburgh Penguins out of the doldrums of last-place finishes to the heights of a Stanley Cup championship in 1992. Meanwhile, young superstar Sidney Crosby got his Jagr in 2006 when the Pens finally got Evegni Malkin, number 71. They had drafted him in 2004 but had to wait two years to get him from Russia. (Author's collection)

Number 71, Evgeni Malkin, may have been a great addition alongside Sidney Crosby, but make no mistake: Malkin is a superstar in his own right and not a second banana to Crosby. In his career to this point, Malkin has captured the Calder Trophy as rookie of the year, the Conn Smythe as playoff MVP, and the Hart Trophy in 2012 as NHL league MVP. (Author's collection)

After starring for the University of Notre Dame where he scored 32 goals in his final two seasons, Bryan Rust went to the Pens AHL club in Wilkes-Barre. Selected by the Pittsburgh Penguins in the third round of the 1980 draft, Rust did not appear to be a future Penguin star until he scored two goals in the seventh game of the 2016 Eastern Conference Finals to send Pittsburgh to the Finals with a 2–1 win. (Courtesy of Fighting Irish Media)

He may have had his problems in recent Penguin postseason history, but in 2009 Marc-Andre Fleury, pictured above, was at his best. Fleury won all 16 games for the Pens on their way to their third Stanley Cup championship, and with a second left in Game Seven of the Finals against Detroit, he made a spectacular save against the Wings' Niklas Lidstrom to preserve the 2–1 championship victory. (Author's collection)

There is no greater privilege for a hockey player then being given the chance to lift the Stanley Cup in honor of the championship their team just won. Sidney Crosby was given the honor for the second time in his career, matching him with the man considered one of the top five players in the history of the game, Mario Lemieux. (Author's collection)

At six foot three, 195 pounds, Evgeni Malkin is not only a talented scorer but a powerful presence on the ice. In 2009 Malkin showed the hockey world just how special he was with a league-leading 36 points in the playoffs, capturing the Conn Smythe Award as playoff MVP, which he shows to an ecstatic Penguins crowd. Against Carolina in the conference finals, Malkin was unstoppable, scoring six goals in the four-game sweep. (Photo courtesy of Vivian Finoli)

The Consol Energy Center opened its doors on October 7, 2010, in a contest against their cross-state rivals, the Philadelphia Flyers, where they lost 3–2. Since moving there, the Penguins have recorded 418 consecutive sellouts. After six years, the facility finally played host to a Stanley Cup final series. Pittsburgh emerged victorious, and as the team decorated the front of the building in celebration of the championship. (Author's collection)

A fifth-round pick of the Pittsburgh Penguins in 1998 out of Boston College, defense-man Rob Scuderi eventually became a very effective stay-at-home defenseman for the team. His defensive play in the 2009 Stanley Cup playoffs was one of the main reasons the franchise was able to capture its third Stanley Cup championship. (Courtesy of Boston College Athletics)

For the better part of their first 23 seasons, the Pittsburgh Penguins were the laughingstock of the National Hockey League. The 1990–91 season changed all that when the team captured its first Stanley Cup championship, a moment that no Penguins fan would have ever imagined. When this photo was taken of banners on the ceiling of the Consol Energy Center, they had won two more. They gained their fourth championship in 2016. (Author's collection)

Considered widely as the second-greatest player in Penguins history behind Mario Lemieux, number 87, Sidney Crosby, has had a spectacular career. While only 28 years old in 2015, Crosby has scored the gold medal–clinching goal for Canada in the 2010 Winter Olympics on top of capturing two Hart Trophies as league MVP and two Art Ross Trophies as the top scorer in the National Hockey League. (Author's collection)

One of the greatest left wings in team history, Kevin Stevens was a key offensive scoring threat on the Penguins Stanley Cup champions in the early 1990s. He scored over 40 goals in four consecutive seasons, netting career highs of 55 and 54 during the 1991–92 and 1992–93 campaigns. (Courtesy of Boston College Athletics)

When fellow superstar Sidney Crosby was sidelined with a concussion in 2011–12, Evgeni Malkin came to the forefront, proving that when it came to talk about the best player in the NHL, he should be included in the conversation. Malkin led the league in scoring with 109 points, while scoring 50 goals for the first time. For his efforts, he was awarded the Hart Trophy as league MVP. (Author's collection)

A star at the University of Massachusetts-Amherst, where he was captain, Conor Sheary was an undrafted free agent when he signed with the Penguins AHL affiliate in Wilkes-Barre in 2015. While he showed flashes of potential with the Baby Penguins, no one would have guessed he would have scored one of the most important goals in Pittsburgh Penguins history, netting a goal in overtime of Game Two of the Stanley Cup Finals against San Jose, leading his team to a 2–1 victory. (Courtesy of Thom Kendall and UMass Athletics)

#21

What Could Have Been

Fourteen years before Mario Lemieux first donned a Penguin uniform and began his journey to becoming the greatest player in franchise history, there was another French-Canadian star who appeared destined to lead the franchise to many championships.

Michel Briere wasn't a top draft pick, nor did he have the size to project that he was going to be an NHL superstar. Standing at just five feet ten inches and weighing only 165 pounds, he was the Pens' third-round pick in the 1969 amateur draft. Despite his diminutive size, Briere was a lightning quick, highly skilled player who had netted 129 goals and 191 assists in just 100 games with the Shawinigan Bruins of the Quebec Major Junior Hockey League.

While his size dropped him into the third round of the NHL entry draft, when he hit the ice for the Penguins in 1969, his speed and skill had scouts and fans alike salivating. Many felt once he reached his potential, he could be counted among the game's elite and would become a pivotal part of Pittsburgh's hopes for a championship-contending franchise.

Briere started off slowly, playing for nearly a month before scoring his first NHL goal, but as the campaign went on, he started showing what talent he had while leading the three-year-old franchise to a second-place finish in the Western Division. The rookie scored 12 goals and collected 44 points in a solid first campaign, but would take his game to the next level as the Penguins entered the Stanley Cup playoffs for the first time.

Pittsburgh's first-round opponent would be the Oakland Seals, who finished the season in fourth place, six points behind the Pens. Despite finishing so close in the standings, the Penguins began to dominate the series. Behind a stifling defense, Pittsburgh opened up a three-games-to-none lead, only allowing four goals along the way. The Penguins would have the opportunity to eliminate Oakland in a Game Four encounter at the Oakland-Alameda County Coliseum Arena.

With their season on the line, the Seals were aggressive from the onset. Before a minuscule crowd of 5,299, Penguins defenseman Bryan "Bugsy" Watson was sent off 1:17 into the game for interference, giving the home team its first power-play opportunity of the evening. Oakland peppered Pittsburgh goalie Les Binkley with several shots before defenseman Carol Vadnais beat the Penguin netminder with a 50-foot slap shot for a 1–0 lead.

Five minutes later, the Pens struck back. Thirty-eight-year-old defenseman Jim Morrison rifled a slap shot at Seals goalie Gary Smith. Smith stopped the shot as he slid down onto the ice but was unable to pull in the rebound. Left wing Dean Prentice, who led Pittsburgh with 26 goals during the regular season, put the rebound over Smith to tie the score.

While Prentice was a hero for the Pens in the first period, early in the second he cost the team the lead, being pulled off for what was described by the *Pittsburgh Post-Gazette* hockey writer Jimmy Jordan as a "somewhat debatable" hook.[1] With Prentice in the box, Vadnais broke in on Binkley and once again beat the Pens' netminder to give Oakland back the lead.

But just as before, Pittsburgh quickly struck back. Two minutes later, Briere showed his brilliance by taking the puck away from two Seals in the corner and finding defenseman Bob Woytowich with a pass at the blue line. Woytowich ripped a slap shot past Smith to make it 2–2 in what proved to be the final goal of regulation.

The defenses took control of the contest after that, and the game tumbled into overtime. The Penguins dominated play early in the extra session, out-shooting the Seals 5–2, setting up the moment in which Briere showcased his incredible talent in a clutch situation. Jean Pronovost fed a perfect pass to Val Fonteyne, who skated toward the goal, drawing out Smith, who went out to poke-check the puck away. The Pens' left wing then filtered a pass to Briere, who broke in and masterfully slid the puck into the open net from a sharp angle, not only to score the first overtime goal in franchise history but to give Pittsburgh its initial series win.

It seemed like a moment that would signify the turning point of Briere's great career. Even after the St. Louis Blues beat the Penguins in the next round, Briere looked like a star in the making. Unfortunately, it all came to an end a month later. While driving back to Quebec to marry his fiancée, Briere was involved in a single-car accident and suffered severe head trauma. He spent

11 months in a coma before passing away exactly one year and one day after he scored what would prove to be the most dramatic goal of his career.

His number 21 was retired and today hangs from the rafters of the Consol Energy Center, a reminder of what might have been.

BOX SCORE

Teams	1	2	3	OT	F
Pittsburgh	1	1	0	1	3
Oakland	1	1	0	0	2

Per	Team	Goal (Assist)	Time
1	Oakland	Vadnais 1 (Marshall)	2:34
1	Pittsburgh	Prentice 1 (Morrison, Schock)	7:37
2	Oakland	Vadnais 2 (Hicke, Roberts)	4:34
2	Pittsburgh	Woytowich 1 (Briere)	6:22
OT	Pittsburgh	Briere 1 (Fonteyne, Pronovost)	8:28

Team	Goalie	Saves	Goals
Pittsburgh	Binkley	27	2
Oakland	Smith	30	3

Shots	1	2	3	OT	T
Pittsburgh	8	9	9	7	33
Oakland	8	8	11	2	29

#20

Survival of the Fittest

In the latter part of the twenty-first century's first decade, the National Hockey League reportedly considered changing its overtime rule for the Stanley Cup playoffs. After the first overtime, the proposal was to take one man off the ice and have the teams play four on four. The idea was to open up the offense and reduce the chance for extended games that some felt hurt the television ratings and adversely affected the health of those who participated in such elongated contests.

The other side of the argument was that longer games created classic games. They became the ultimate test of endurance, a sort of survival of the fittest. In the first round of the 1996 Stanley Cup playoffs, the Pittsburgh Penguins and the Washington Capitals created a perfect example of this argument.

While the Penguins had posted a superior regular-season record, the teams had a rich playoff history built on a handful of classic matchups. Game Four in '96 would add to their legacy.

With Mario Lemieux and Jaromir Jagr, two of the greatest players ever to take the ice, Pittsburgh led the league in offense that year, netting 362 goals—35 more than the next-highest tally. Lemieux and Jagr finished one-two in goals scored (69 and 62, respectively) and points (161 and 149). Meanwhile, the gritty, defensive-oriented Capitals had scored 128 fewer goals than Pittsburgh but were third best in the league in goals allowed. The Caps surprised everyone by finding an offensive attack that had been missing all season, combining for 11 goals to capture the first two games of the series at Civic Arena.

The Pens bounced back to take Game Three in Washington, but history was against them for Game Four. Only 12 times in league history had the visiting team won the first four games of a playoff series.

Washington took advantage of an early Pittsburgh penalty to take a 1–0 lead late in the first period on a shot past Pittsburgh goal Tom Barrasso, and the situation looked even more dire for the Penguins when Barrasso remained in the locker room with muscle spasms after the first intermission. Backup Ken Wregget replaced him in goal as the second period began, and Lemieux and the Pittsburgh offense did their best to take control of the game, dominating the first 10 minutes of the period. Capital goalie Olaf Kolzig kept the Pens off the board and the Capitals on top, although he had a little luck as the period went on. Lemieux was denied on a great opportunity when he hit the post with the shot and then was robbed by the Washington goalie moments later on a great save off a shorthanded shot. The missed opportunities hurt even more when the Capitals' Peter Bondra gave Washington a 2–0 lead 10 seconds after Kolzig's big save.

Pittsburgh was able to cut the lead in half with less than two minutes left in the second when Jagr took a pass from Ron Francis and beat Kolzig for a shorthanded goal.

The Caps quickly took the momentum right back. After the Capitals' Todd Krygier took what he felt was a cheap shot at him, Lemieux lost his temper, first slashing Krygier and then jumping on top of him throwing punches. The Penguins' future Hall of Famer was given a double minor penalty and an automatic game misconduct for instigating a fight.

Now facing a four-minute disadvantage with their best player out for the game, the Pens rose to the occasion, allowing only three shots on the Washington power play. Then, eight minutes into the third period, Petr Nedved ripped a shot past Kolzig eight minutes into the third to tie the score.

Pittsburgh dominated the rest of the period, outshooting Washington 19–5, but Kolzig remained tough, shutting out the Penguins the rest of the way. Regulation ended, but as it turned out, the game wasn't even halfway over.

The Capitals controlled the first extra period, outshooting Pittsburgh 14–3, but it wasn't until the second when the first real scoring opportunity arose. Nedved came close to ending the game when he rifled a backhander that appeared would beat the Washington goalie, but Kolzig stopped it to keep the game tied.

With less than five minutes left in the second overtime, the Caps had their best opportunity to take the game and a solid lead in the series when Penguin defenseman Chris Tamer pulled the net off the moorings—which, in a playoff game, results in a penalty shot for the opposing team. Washington center Joe Juneau took the shot for Washington, but Wregget was up to the challenge and stopped the puck, keeping the score even at two. The contest then tumbled into a third overtime. Then a fourth.

After being outshot 37–12 in the three extra sessions, Pittsburgh changed the momentum in the fourth. But even then, the Penguins were stymied by Kolzig.

As clocks ticked past 2 a.m., it looked like the game might surpass the longest ever in NHL history: a 1936 match between the Detroit Red Wings and Montreal Maroons, which took six overtimes to settle. But just before the teams could begin a fifth overtime session, Nedved ended the affair at the 19:15 mark with his second power play of the game to give the Pens an exhausting 3–2 victory that evened the series at two.

It was a classic contest defined by strong goalie play, with Kolzig stopping 62 shots and Wregget handling 53 of the 54 that came his way after he was thrust into the spotlight. More importantly, the contest demonstrated why the league should leave the overtime rules in the playoffs alone.

It was the third-longest game in NHL postseason history and the longest for the franchise at that point in its history, to be surpassed four years later when the Pens lost a five-period overtime contest to the Flyers.

And like so many of the classic overtime games in league playoff history, it became more like a struggle than a contest, symbolizing a survival of the fittest.

BOX SCORE

Teams	1	2	3	OT	OT	OT	OT	F
Pittsburgh	0	1	1	0	0	0	1	3
Washington	1	1	0	0	0	0	0	2

Per	Team	Goal (Assist)	Time
1	Washington	Pivonka 3 (Hunter, Gonchar)	13:50
2	Washington	Bondra 3 (Juneau, Brunette)	7:36
2	Pittsburgh	Jagr 1 (Francis)	18:42
3	Pittsburgh	Nedved 5 (Daigneault, Zubov)	8:00
4OT	Pittsburgh	Nedved 6 (Zubov, Jagr)	19:15

Team	Goalie	Saves	Goals
Pittsburgh	Barrasso	8	1
Pittsburgh	Wregget	53	1
Washington	Kolzig	62	3

Shots	1	2	3	OT	OT	OT	OT	T
Pittsburgh	16	7	19	3	4	5	11	65
Washington	9	7	5	14	12	11	5	63

#19

PENGUINS 3, NEW JERSEY DEVILS 2
MAY 2, 1999

The Goal That Saved Pittsburgh

One of the few constants for the Pittsburgh Penguins in their pre-Consol Energy Center days was that every few years the team would be in dire financial straits. As the twentieth century was coming to an end, the Pens situation was as bad as it had ever been.

Over the course of his ownership, Howard Baldwin made some questionable business decisions, negotiating away quite a few revenue sources in order to gain the capital to maintain the team. Add to the mix skyrocketing salaries and several questionable contract decisions in order to keep the base of his successful team together, and you had a recipe for financial disaster.

In 1999 it was all coming to a head as the Penguins were taking on the New Jersey Devils in the first round of the Stanley Cup playoffs. It was thought to be essential for Pittsburgh to win the series in order to get to the next round to play more home games and generate more revenue. In fact, there were rumors that if they lost the first-round series, Baldwin would have no choice but to sell the Penguins or move them to another city.

If the rumors were true, then the Penguins looked like an endangered species as the series unfolded. The Pens started off strong, winning two of the first three in the best-of-seven series, but after losing Games Four and Five, Pittsburgh was on the verge of elimination—perhaps permanently. Luckily for Pittsburgh coach Kevin Constantine, star Jaromir Jagr would return to the lineup after missing the previous four games with a groin pull. Though he would be far from 100 percent healthy, Jagr would try to provide the spark the Penguins desperately needed.

Only 15,367 fans, about 2,000 short of Igloo capacity, showed up for what could potentially have been the last playoff game in franchise history. And

125

those who came were discouraged early when the Devils surged ahead with the first goal of the game at the 12:04 mark.

Martin Straka tied the game early in the second period, and the teams battled into what would prove to be a fateful third period tied at one. Midway through the final 20 minutes, with Pittsburgh's Alex Kovalev in the penalty box for cross checking, New Jersey's Jason Arnott rifled a shot that hit off the right leg of Scott Niedermayer, skidding past Barrasso and into the net to give the Devils the lead once again.

With time running out, the Penguins' chances looked grim. They were not only facing arguably the best goaltender in the game in Martin Brodeur but also a stifling New Jersey defense. As the clock ticked down, the Penguins needed a miracle.

In times like these they usually relied on Jagr to save the day. He had intended to play only in power-play situations but wound up logging more ice time than all but two players in the game. Even though he had pushed the limits, Jagr later said he was only at about 60 percent and was struggling to skate fluidly in open space.

With just over two minutes left in regulation, Pittsburgh's German Titov broke toward the New Jersey goal before Devils defenseman Scott Stevens poke-checked the puck from Titov behind the net. The Pens' center chased the puck and then flipped a perfect pass to Jagr, who scored to tie the game at two.

It was an incredible moment for Pittsburgh and Jagr, but there was still more work to be done. The game tumbled into overtime, and after eight minutes of play in the extra session, Jagr stepped up once again. Martin Straka was breaking into the Devils' zone with Jagr, on his right on a two-on-one break. As the lone defender leaned toward him, Straka passed the puck to Jagr, who put a one-timer above Brodeur with 11:01 left in the overtime to give the Pens the much-needed victory and tie the series at three games apiece.

The goal turned out to be bigger than the Penguin fans imagined at the time. The team ended up beating New Jersey in Game Seven two nights later to win the series and get a financial lifeline with another series against the Toronto Maple Leafs. Jagr seemed to understand the importance of his score. "That was probably my best game ever," the injured Penguin superstar would say. "My most important for sure. I'll probably never score a goal that important. Probably if I hadn't scored, the team wouldn't be in Pittsburgh right now."[1]

While it was thought that the Jagr goal was the financial boon that Baldwin needed to keep the team afloat, a few months later the team did indeed declare bankruptcy. Luckily, another Penguin great stepped in to save the day when Mario Lemieux, in fact, saved the Penguins by heading a group that purchased the team.

While it may not have exactly saved the franchise as first thought, Jagr's goal was an important factor in one of the greatest comebacks in the team's history.

BOX SCORE

Teams	1	2	3	OT	F
New Jersey	1	0	1	0	2
Pittsburgh	0	1	1	1	3

Per	Team	Goal (Assist)	Time
1	New Jersey	Brylin 3 (Holik, Odelein)	12:04
2	Pittsburgh	Straka 5 (Kovalev, Titov)	6:44
3	New Jersey	Niedermayer 1 (Arnot, Sykora)	4:34
3	Pittsburgh	Jagr 1 (Titov, Kovalev)	17:48
OT	Pittsburgh	Jagr 2 (Straka, Moran)	8:59

Team	Goalie	Saves	Goals
New Jersey	Brodeur	25	3
Pittsburgh	Barrasso	25	2

Shots	1	2	3	OT	T
New Jersey	15	4	5	3	27
Pittsburgh	7	7	10	4	28

#18

PENGUINS 10, NEW YORK RANGERS 4
APRIL 9, 1993

The Streak

Coming off two consecutive Stanley Cup championships, the Pittsburgh Penguins had already cemented their place in NHL history. The Pens' success only continued as the 1992–93 campaign was coming to an end, as they'd already clinched a playoff spot and were on their way to the Patrick Division title. With 18 games remaining, they'd have the opportunity to rest some of their top players to make sure they went into the playoffs refreshed and ready to defend their crown. But just when they were about to relax, something strange began to happen. The two-time defending champs found another avenue into the record book as they began a winning streak that had never been equaled in the NHL.

It began with a closely fought victory over the Bruins on March 9, followed by two more one-goal victories. By the time Pittsburgh stretched it to five with a lopsided 9–3 victory against the Philadelphia Flyers, they were playing their best hockey of the year. Still, eclipsing the league record of 15 consecutive victories set by the 1981–82 New York Islanders didn't seem like a realistic possibility.

The Penguins continued their string of victories, and following a 10–2 rout of the Hartford Whalers, the streak had reached 12, and now the record was within reach. Wins at Quebec and New Jersey brought the Pens within one game of tying the mark, and a gritty overtime victory against the Montreal Canadiens tied the record.

The next contest would be played at Madison Square Garden against the New York Rangers—ironically, the site of the Penguins' last defeat more than a month before. Unlike Pittsburgh, New York was not playing well, losing nine of its next 14 games since that victory, and riding a 5–9 record since that game, and everything seemed to be lining up perfectly in Pittsburgh's quest for the record books.

Whether or not they set the record, Penguin captain Mario Lemieux knew that they had already accomplished something special by tying the mark, and that this achievement would further solidify them as one of the best teams in hockey history. "Great teams do that," the future Hall of Famer said. "They go out there and do whatever it takes to win."[1]

At the beginning of the contest, it looked like the underdog Rangers would fight hard enough to prevent the Pens from their date with history. After Pittsburgh's Joe Mullen started the scoring with a shorthanded goal 11 minutes into the game, New York tied it when Adam Graves beat Tom Barrasso for his 35th of the year. Pittsburgh rebounded to score twice, but each time the Rangers battled back to net the equalizer, and the game was tied at three, six minutes into the second period. At that point, the Penguins quickly turned this tight game into a rout.

After scoring his 63rd goal of the year to start the second period, Lemieux completed a hat trick by scoring two more goals before the period came to an end to give Pittsburgh a 5–3 advantage.

Things only got worse for the Rangers in the final period, when the Penguins simply manhandled them, netting four goals in just over seven minutes, two by Mullen as he also netted a hat trick. When the scoring onslaught was over, Pittsburgh held a 9–3 lead with still over half a period left to play.

With a 16th straight victory now all but certain, Lemieux put a resounding end to this memorable evening when he scored his fifth goal of the night, beating Mike Richter, who replaced Hirsch to start the third. Alexei Kovalev scored a meaningless goal for New York late in the period, but the night, belonged to the Penguins, as they closed out a 10–4 victory.

Coach Scotty Bowman appreciated just how hard it was to achieve such a winning streak. "It's hard because there are ties and there are good teams," he said. "We've got a lot of parity in the league now. I think that says a lot about the record."[2]

Pittsburgh would stretch the streak to 17 games before tying New Jersey in the final game of the regular season. While they fell short of winning their third straight Stanley Cup championship, the streak defined the 1992–93 season and has endured, even when it was threatened in 2013 when the Penguins won 15 straight.

But that team fell short of the streak, as have any number of other winning streaks since—proving just how remarkable the record and the team that set it truly were.

BOX SCORE

Teams	1	2	3	F
Pittsburgh	2	3	5	10
New York	2	1	1	4

Per	Team	Goal (Assist)	Time
1	Pittsburgh	Mullen 30	11:02
1	New York	Graves 35	15:25
1	Pittsburgh	Murphy 22 (Stevens, Tocchet)	16:24
1	New York	McIntyre 3 (Erixon, Wells)	16:41
2	Pittsburgh	Lemieux 63 (U. Samuelsson)	4:43
2	New York	Amonte 32 (Tikkanen, Cirella)	6:01
2	Pittsburgh	Lemieux 64 (Francis, Tocchet)	4:14
2	Pittsburgh	Lemieux 65 (Barrasso)	16:05
3	Pittsburgh	Mullen 31 (Jagr, U. Samuelsson)	1:52
3	Pittsburgh	Lemieux 66 (Tocchet, Stevens)	4:14
3	Pittsburgh	Jagr 34 (Barrasso)	8:14
3	Pittsburgh	Mullen 32 (Francis)	9:21
3	Pittsburgh	Lemieux 67 (Stevens, Jennings)	11:15
3	New York	Kovalev 20	18:40

Team	Goalie	Saves	Goals
Pittsburgh	Barrasso	21	4
New York	Hirsch	20	5
New York	Richter	10	5

Shots	1	2	3	T
Pittsburgh	17	8	15	40
New York	9	5	11	25

#17

Cancel the Parade

Normally a team must win four games in a best-of-seven championship series before it can start planning the celebration that follows. The parade, the trip to the White House, and the ensuing parties all become priorities once the trophy has been awarded. In the 1991 Stanley Cup Finals that pitted the Pittsburgh Penguins against the Minnesota North Stars, rumors flew that several North Star players were so confident after they took an unexpected two-games-to one lead that the plans for a celebration had already been put in motion.

Minnesota split the first two games at the Civic Arena to wrestle away home-ice advantage from the Penguins, and, after an impressive 3–1 victory at home in Game Three, they felt very comfortable that they would soon hoist the Stanley Cup for the first time. This confidence was justified based on their incredible run of success at the Met Center, a small, intimate facility in Minneapolis that produced an extremely loud intimidating presence. After all, Minnesota had won eight consecutive playoff games and was 20–2–2 in its previous 24 home games.

After Game Three, articles appeared in the Minnesota papers about the championship parade that was being planned by city officials. Yet the news didn't really affect the Pens' psyche and was dismissed as reporters just trying to print controversial text. What did get the Penguins' attention was another article about how the North Star players were looking forward to meeting President George H. W. Bush at the White House after winning the cup. Minnesota left wing Basil McRae said, "Tell George I'm Canadian, but that I'll still try and vote for him. Count me in."[1] Penguin defenseman Gordie Roberts reminded everyone, "They don't award the Cup after two wins."[2]

By the start of Game Four, the inspired Pens had heard enough about how visiting teams couldn't win at the Met and how fabulous the victory parades and White House visit would be. The Minnesota hockey writers and North Star players had woken up a sleeping giant who was about to show them what a mistake their overconfidence had been.

Pittsburgh came on to the ice angry to start the game, and before the sold-out throng of 15,378 had a chance to settle in, the dreams of Stanley Cups and parades were a distant memory.

Pittsburgh left wing Kevin Stevens started the proceedings with an unassisted goal 58 seconds into the game to give the Penguins a quick 1–0 lead. Less than two minutes later, Ron Francis took a pass from Joe Mullen and slapped a shot past Jon Casey to stretch the Pens advantage to two. Twenty-two seconds after that, Mario Lemieux notched his 14th of the postseason to make the score 3–0 in a game that wasn't even three minutes old.

Minnesota's players and fans were stunned. But the North Stars settled down to keep the game from being a rout, cutting the margin to 3–1 late in the first period. Then, midway through the second, Pittsburgh veteran Bryan Trottier restored the Penguins' three-goal advantage when he pushed a backhander past Casey. With the Pens in control, they began their own parade of sorts—to the penalty box. Six Pittsburgh penalties led to four power-play opportunities for the North Stars, who scored twice to transform a rout into a nail-biter as the second period wound down.

The North Stars had seized the momentum and nearly tied the score when Brian Bellows had a point-blank shot from close range. Luckily though, Pens goalie Tom Barrasso came to the rescue, making a phenomenal save to keep Pittsburgh in front going into the last period of regulation.

As the teams began a tense third period, Pittsburgh's discipline issues arose again when Troy Loney was sent off with just under seven minutes remaining for a five-minute major high-sticking penalty that would put Minnesota on the power play for nearly the rest of the contest.

After Pittsburgh's three-goal outburst in the first three minutes, the Stars had completely controlled the action, outshooting the Pens 38–24. While the odds were beginning to look brighter for a White House visit with the Stanley Cup for the Stars, the Pittsburgh penalty kill unit took over, completely shutting down Minnesota, allowing no shots on goal for the first 3:49 of the five-minute stretch. At that point, Casey interfered with Phil Bourque, resulting in a Minnesota penalty and putting the teams back at equal strength.

Bourque ended up putting the game away with an empty-net goal with 15 seconds left, securing a much needed 5–3 win for the Penguins. With the victory, they'd not only taken back home-ice advantage for the series but had also halted all talk of the parade plans the North Stars and their fans had considered a certainty.

BOX SCORE

Teams	1	2	3	F
Pittsburgh	3	1	1	5
Minnesota	1	2	0	3

Per	Team	Goal (Assist)	Time
1	Pittsburgh	Stevens 16	:58
1	Pittsburgh	Francis 5 (Stevens, Mullen)	2:36
1	Pittsburgh	Lemieux 14 (Recchi, Murphy)	2:58
1	Minnesota	Gagner 10 (Bellows, Dahlen)	18:22
2	Pittsburgh	Trottier 3 (Errey, Jagr)	9:55
2	Minnesota	Propp 8 (Gagner)	13:10
2	Minnesota	Modano 8 (Propp, Gagner)	18:25
3	Pittsburgh	Bourque 6 (Mullen, Lemieux)	19:45

Team	Goalie	Saves	Goals
Pittsburgh	Barrasso	35	3
Minnesota	Casey	23	4

Shots	1	2	3	T
Pittsburgh	13	5	6	24
Minnesota	14	17	7	38

#16

The Called Shot

The date was October 1, 1932, Game Three of the World Series, the Chicago Cubs against the New York Yankees at the friendly confines of Wrigley Field. It was a day that lives on in the annals of Major League Baseball history as the game Babe Ruth called his famous shot.

The game was tied at four in the top of the fifth inning; Joe Sewell was on first base and the mighty Babe was coming to the plate. The Cubs' bench was abusive toward the Bambino, and he kept pointing at them. The count was two balls and two strikes when, as legend has it, Ruth pointed toward center field, calling where he was going to hit the ball. Remarkably the next pitch was crushed by the Bambino and fell exactly where the Babe supposedly pointed to, over the center field wall, putting New York on top 6–4 as they went on to win the series.

Without the intensity of social media in the 1930s, no one knows if Ruth actually called his shot, but in Game Two of the 2016 Stanley Cup Finals the NHL had its own version of the legendary moment, one that happened without question. It wasn't sexy; hell, the man who called the shot didn't even score the winning goal. That man is the second greatest player in the Penguins history, Sidney Crosby. He saw a potential opportunity, communicated that opportunity to his two teammates before the play, and watched it work out exactly as he called it. It was the called shot, second edition.

Another difference with the Bambino-called shot was that it required the efforts of three men, working in harmony to create one of the franchise's most memorable moments: Crosby; their top defenseman, Kris Letang; and Conor Sheary, a young rookie who a few months before was known only to close friends, family, and devoted minor league hockey fans. Each had individual stories of redemption that helped the Penguins get to this point of the season.

After suffering through the effects of a severe concussion for the better part of two years, the Penguins captain was looking like the player he used to be, enjoying two superior campaigns in 2012–13 and 2013–14 when he not only captured his second scoring title but was awarded his second Hart Memorial Trophy, symbolic of the league's MVP.

Surprisingly at 27 years old, his career started to decline during the post-season when he scored only one goal in 13 games. The malaise continued into the next season with only 84 points, his lowest mark ever when playing a full season. Crosby continued his woes, contributing a mere two goals against the Rangers in the first round of the playoffs.

Continuing his struggles in 2015–16, by mid-season the talk shows in Pittsburgh were discussing not whether to retire his number when he left the game but whether to trade him immediately. Luckily for the Penguin captain, along came coach Mike Sullivan. Under his new coach, Crosby thrived, becoming the leader he once was as his scoring touch returned. Remarkably, Crosby went from being left off the All-Star team to finishing second in the Hart Trophy race.

Letang was a wonderfully talented defenseman whom general manager Ray Shero had signed to an eight-year $58 million contract in the summer of 2013. Not long afterward it had looked like a huge mistake as Letang played poorly with a -8 plus-minus in 2013–14 before suffering a concussion and eventually a stroke in February 2014. The contract was once thought to be foolhardy for a salary cap–strapped franchise. Eventually, it turned into a steal as Letang rebounded in 2014–15 before also responding to Sullivan's leadership that helped him turn into one of the most dominant defensemen in the league.

Sheary had the least pedigree of the three. He was a star winger for the University of Massachusetts but was undrafted after his senior season. Signed as a minor league free agent by Pittsburgh, he showed potential in Wilkes-Barre with 11 points in 15 games during the 2013–14 Calder Cup playoff before netting 20 goals in his first full professional regular season. Sullivan gave Sheary a chance to shine at the NHL level, not only bringing him up but putting him on a line with Crosby and Patric Hornqvist in the postseason. He was a small yet fast player who used his speed and grit to go through defenses and get to loose pucks the way the team hadn't been doing under former coach Mike Johnston.

It was these three who would combine on the memorable play, a play that if not for a fluke goal late by San Jose never would have had the chance to happen. The Sharks had been made a slight favorite by most media outlets but had lost the first contest on an overtime goal by Nick Bonino. Since 44 of the previous 49 teams in the Stanley Cup Finals had gone on to win the cup after taking a two-game-to-none advantage, it was imperative that San Jose find a way to win Game Two.

As much as they needed the victory, it was Pittsburgh that dominated play early on, outshooting San Jose 23–10 in the first two periods. The only thing that kept the Sharks in the game was the stellar goaltending of Martin Jones. He kept the game scoreless until 8:20 of the second when Bonino launched a shot at Jones that appeared to beat him to the glove side. Not wanting to take a chance of the puck veering away, Phil Kessel made sure it went in by deflecting it past the Shark netminder, giving the Pens the 1–0 lead.

While San Jose finally seemed to get some momentum in the final period, they were unable to beat Matt Murray. It appeared as if Pittsburgh was going to escape with the shutout victory. The aggressive forechecking that they utilized so perfectly in these playoffs was helping to keep the Sharks off the board. Finally, with a little over four minutes left, San Jose defenseman Justin Braun took a seemingly innocent shot from a difficult angle that hit the right goal post, deflected, and quieted the raucous Consol Center crowd. The contest was tied.

Outplaying the Pens the rest of regulation, Pittsburgh held on to send the game into overtime. Luckily for the sold-out throng, the Penguins had become a team that found a way to come back when things were going against them. This contest was no different.

With 2:30 gone in the extra period, there was a face-off in the Sharks' end with Crosby in the circle. It was at this point he set up the play that has become franchise lore. Pulling Sheary and Letang together before this all-important face-off, a confident Crosby told Letang to expect the pass; then he told Sheary to go to the wall and find the soft spot in the defense where he would get the pass from Letang. The play sounded simple but would be very difficult to pull off. As he expected, Crosby won the draw. He then rifled the pass to Letang as the rookie was finding the soft spot in the defense. Sheary found it and took the called pass from Letang, sending a shot over Jones's glove to give Pittsburgh the exciting 2–1 victory and a two-game lead in the series.

A joyous Crosby quipped after the contest, "I call 25 faceoffs a night. I got 24 wrong tonight."[1] It was the 25th he got right, the called shot that was as pivotal to the Penguins winning a championship as Ruth's was to the Yankees some 84 years earlier.

BOX SCORE

Team	1	2	3	OT	F
San Jose	0	0	1	0	1
Pittsburgh	0	1	0	1	2

Per	Team	Goal (Assist)	Time
2	Pittsburgh	Kessel 10 (Bonino, Hagelin)	8:20
3	San Jose	Braun 1 (Couture, Ward)	15:55
OT	Pittsburgh	Sheary 4 (Letang, Crosby)	2:35

Team	Goalie	Saves	Goals
San Jose	Jones	28	2
Pittsburgh	Murray	21	1

Team	1	2	3	OT	T
San Jose	6	5	9	2	22
Pittsburgh	11	12	6	1	30

#15

The Pride of Notre Dame

When you think of the greatest legends in the celebrated history of Notre Dame athletics, the ones that quickly come to mind are those that played on the gridiron, the place where this Indiana school had enjoyed its greatest glory. The names Rockne, Montana, Gipp, Bertelli, Lujack, Lattner, Hart, Huarte, Honung, and Brown spring to mind quickly. On May 26, 2016, another Notre Dame athlete came to the national sports consciousness unexpectedly, scoring both goals in Game Seven of the Eastern Conference championship, which sent the Pittsburgh Penguins to the Stanley Cup Finals for the first time in seven years. His name was Bryan Rust, and on this day he truly was the pride of Notre Dame.

It's understandable why a member of the Fighting Irish hockey team is not usually part of the conversation when discussing the history of this iconic university; after all, the program has not been among the schools most successful. Its most notable players include Jim Crowley, a goaltender in the early 1920s, and Angelo Bertelli, who scored four goals in a game. Crowley and Bertelli were not Irish legends because of their hockey prowess. Crowley was a member of coach Knute Rockne's famous Four Horsemen backfield (in fact, in was Rockne who told Crowley to give up hockey), and Bertelli is the same Bertelli who captured the Heisman Trophy. So unimpressive was the Fighting Irish hockey team that as late as 1983 is was downgraded from varsity to a club sport.

Eventually, Notre Dame hockey took hold in the twenty-first century making, the NCAA field eight times since 2004, including Frozen Four appearances in 2008 and 2011, the latter of which included Rust among its ranks.

A third-round draft pick of the Penguins in 2010, Rust scored 43 times in 161 games during his Irish career, including 32 over his final two seasons. When general manager Jim Rutherford and coach Mike Sullivan were looking to upgrade the team's speed and grit, they looked no further than the Pontiac, Michigan, native who had been a sparkplug at the Pens AHL affiliate in Wilkes-Barre.

Not known for his scoring ability as much as for his speed and his aggressiveness in getting to the puck, Rust scored only four goals in the 41 games he played for Pittsburgh during this campaign and five in 55 career NHL games. Therefore, it came as quite a shock to most that he became very important offensively to the club in the 2016 Stanley Cup playoffs. If one had known how tough the Notre Dame product was, perhaps they wouldn't have been surprised. He dealt with a bad speech impediment all of his life, but it never held him back. It was something he shared with a former Wilkes-Barre teammate, his brother Matt. "It's kind of something we've grown up with together and just dealt with. I've had a lot of people around me that have been really supportive with it. Sometimes, it's not so bad. Sometimes, it's really bad. It's just one of those things I've just kind of learned to deal with."[1] With everything the young winger had been through in his life, having the performance of a lifetime when his team needed one most seemed feasible.

It had been a tough series against the Tampa Bay Lightning, despite the fact the Penguins' opponent had played without their superstar scorer Steven Stamkos, who spent two months on the bench while dealing with a blood clot issue, and without starting goalie Ben Bishop, who was hurt early in the first contest. Winning Games Four and Five, Tampa had put itself in a position to end the Penguins' season at home in the sixth game. With their surprising season about to end, Pittsburgh played its best game of the series, defeating the Lightning 5–2 to force a seventh and deciding game at the Consol Center.

Tampa coach Jon Cooper had a trick up his sleeve for this decisive contest—unleashing Stamkos on the Penguin in hopes of reviving the team's offense. It was a move that almost paid off in the second period when the all-star broke in on rookie goaltender Matt Murray. Murray calmly stopped the shot as he and Lightning netminder Andrei Vasilevskiy were dominating the game.

Despite the fact that Pittsburgh seemed to be getting the better of the play, the game was scoreless after the first period. Rust quickly ended the scoreless affair in the second. Chris Kunitz fed his young linemate in front of Vasilevskiy, who promptly lifted a shot past the Lightning goalie's glove for the early lead.

The Penguins not only continued to do well but they began to take control of the contest in the second period. While they finished with a 21–5 advantage in shots in the second, Jonathan Drouin ripped a shot past Murray midway through the period to tie the score at one. With the series now in peril, the Pens soon proved how tough they and the Notre Dame product had become in this playoff season, as they quickly calmed an anxious Penguin nation.

Thirty seconds later defenseman Ben Lovejoy launched a slap shot wide of the goal. The puck bounced off in front of the net where Rust just happened to be. He poked the puck in a small opening inside Vasilevskiy's arm to put his name beside the likes of Mario Lemieux and Max Talbot as players with the greatest clutch goals in franchise history.

Tampa Bay wasn't the defending Eastern Conference champions because they gave up when the situation seemed tough—and they didn't here. They kept coming at the Penguin net, but Murray and his teammates, who time and time would block shots before they got to him, stayed tough. Pittsburgh ended up outshooting them 39–17 for the game, hanging on for their fifth Eastern Conference title.

Going against the tradition of not touching the Prince of Wales Trophy, a superstitious tradition meant to show that teams are not happy until they win a Stanley Cup, Sidney Crosby and the team picked it up and celebrated in front of their appreciative home crowd. For Rust, it was the pinnacle moment of a satisfying playoff season, one that his fellow alumni at his prestigious alma mater could take pride in. For one day, his name could comfortably be placed among the greatest athletes ever to wear a Fighting Irish uniform.

BOX SCORE

Team	1	2	3	F
Tampa Bay	0	1	0	1
Pittsburgh	0	2	0	2

Per	Team	Goal (Assist)	Time
2	Pittsburgh	Rust 4 (Kunitz, Malkin)	1:55
2	Tampa Bay	Drouin 5 (Flippula, Hedman)	9:36
2	Pittsburgh	Rust 5 (Lovejoy, Malkin)	10:06

Team	Goalie	Saves	Goals
Tampa Bay	Vasilevskiy	37	2
Pittsburgh	Murray	16	1

Shots	1	2	3	T
Tampa Bay	5	5	7	17
Pittsburgh	8	21	10	39

#14

The 15-Year Nightmare

On January 20, 1974, the Pittsburgh Penguins routed the defending Stanley Cup champion Philadelphia Flyers at the Spectrum in downtown Philly. Five different Penguins scored, and Andy Brown, the NHL's last maskless goaltender, fended off 38 Philadelphia shots. Yet the victory garnered little attention in the *Pittsburgh Post-Gazette* the following day, with the story buried beneath summaries of college basketball games. Had the editors at the *Post-Gazette* known the historical significance of the Pens' victory, it likely would have earned a more prominent place.

As it turned out, it would be the last time the Penguins would win in Philadelphia for the next decade and beyond. From 1975 until 1989, the Penguins played 42 games there and lost 39 of them, settling for three ties along the way. It was an amazing, difficult-to-explain phenomenon that caught the attention of the national and local media alike.

Desperate measures were taken to snap the string. On Groundhog Day in 1989 Pittsburgh radio announcers Scott Paulsen and Jimmy Krenn arrived at the Spectrum's press box parading as witch doctors. During the broadcast, they prayed to the "god of Zambonis" and proclaimed that the streak would end. Perhaps the stunt convinced the hockey gods to lift the curse that troubled the team for so long, as they would in fact end one of sports' most curious losing streaks on that evening.

By 1989, the Penguins appeared on the brink of an upsurge, led by budding superstar Mario Lemieux. After missing the playoffs for six consecutive seasons, the club stood at 25–18–4 as it made another trip to Philadelphia, three points in front of their cross-state rivals.

As far as the Penguins had come in 1988–89, the streak still remained alive as the Pens had lost their first two games at the Spectrum that season, both one-goal defeats.

The Pens turned to a former Flyer goalie in the hopes of ending the streak: Wendell Young, whom they'd acquired in the off-season for a third-round draft pick. Even though he was far from the most impressive talent on the Penguins, on this evening he would play a key role.

While only a Penguin for a matter of months, Young knew what an emotional drain this was for the franchise. "The streak is mostly a psychological thing," he said. "You try not to talk about it much, but it's there."[1]

From the outset, Pittsburgh was determined to lift the psychological barrier. Lemieux and Hannan were stopped on breakaways by Flyer goalie Ron Hextall, but shortly after, John Cullen took a pass from Lemieux and scored midway in the first to give the Penguins an early 1–0 lead.

Phil Bourque then netted his 15th of the year to double the Penguin advantage with less than two minutes left in the opening frame, but 44 seconds later, Philadelphia's Ron Sutter cut the lead back to one.

In the past Sutter's goal would have signaled the start of a momentum change that would have obliterated Pittsburgh's attempt to win a game at the Spectrum. But this was a different team on the brink of a different era, and this time the Pens took their game to another level. Early in the second period, after Mario Lemieux hit the post with a shot with Flyer defenseman Mark Howe hanging on him, teammate Bob Errey came to the rescue, sending the rebound past Hextall to make the score 3–1.

With momentum now firmly on their side, the Penguins extended their lead when Robbie Brown scored his 38th goal of the season midway through the second period. With 20 minutes left and determined to extend the streak to 44 games, Philadelphia turned up the heat, constantly muscling through the Pens' defense. Former Penguin sharpshooter Mike Bullard scored to make it 4–2 early in the third and then Bullard and Sutter fired point-blank shots on goal, but both were turned away. Philly left wing Derrick Smith then had another golden opportunity to score but saw his close-range shot hit the post. Suddenly, it seemed like destiny was on Pittsburgh's side.

Before fate could change direction again, Pittsburgh's Dave Hannan hit Dan Quinn with a perfect pass through an over-aggressive Philadelphia defense, and Quinn rifled a shot past Hextall to make it 5–2. Quinn's score cushioned the Penguins when the Flyers scored one of their own just over a minute later. Down the stretch, Young would not let his new team down, turning aside 14 of 16 third-period shots, most from close range. And when the final buzzer sounded, Young had accomplished something no goalie had done since Andy Brown 15 years before him—beat the Flyers at the Spectrum.

The 1989 Penguins were laying the groundwork for an impressive future, and coach Gene Ubriaco knew that this was a huge barrier to overcome. "This was a big one," he said afterward. Winger Rob Brown seemed to understand what this meant to the Penguin nation. "You know who I'm happiest for?" Brown quipped. "The fans. A guy like me has only played four or five games in this place. They're the ones who waited."[2]

Brown was right. It was a great moment, one that Penguin fans who had suffered through the 15-year nightmare celebrated. In the *Post-Gazette* the next day, the victory earned all the attention it was due, with the game story placed atop the sports page.

BOX SCORE

Teams	1	2	3	F
Pittsburgh	2	2	1	5
Philadelphia	1	0	2	3

Per	Team	Goal (Assist)	Time
1	Pittsburgh	Cullen 10 (R. Brown, Lemieux)	10:45
1	Pittsburgh	Bourque 15 (Cullen)	18:19
1	Philadelphia	Sutter 18 (Samuelsson, Tocchet)	19:03
2	Pittsburgh	Errey 19 (Lemieux)	7:10
2	Pittsburgh	R. Brown 38 (Loney)	9:53
3	Philadelphia	Bullard 18 (Carkner, Samuelsson)	1:09
3	Pittsburgh	Quinn 26 (Hannan)	6:36
3	Philadelphia	Eklund 11 (Sutter, Tocchet)	7:56

Team	Goalie	Saves	Goals
Pittsburgh	Young	39	3
Philadelphia	Hextall	26	5

Shots	1	2	3	T
Pittsburgh	7	15	9	31
Philadelphia	12	14	16	42

PENGUINS 3, WASHINGTON CAPITALS 1
MAY 1, 1992

Never Say Die

The year 1992 had been a struggle for the Pittsburgh Penguins. After winning the franchise's first Stanley Cup the year before, the Penguins found out it wouldn't be as easy the second time around.

Captain Mario Lemieux won the Art Ross Trophy as the league's leading scorer for the third time, but injuries had limited him to only 64 games. Injuries to other key players and the death of the head coach Bob Johnson had made this season even more difficult to endure.

Pittsburgh played below its potential for most of the year, holding a 28–27–8 mark at the end of February. The Penguins put it together in the final two months to finish with 87 points, good enough for third place in the Patrick Division. Their opponent in the first round of the playoffs would be the second-place Washington Capitals, who'd finished 11 points ahead of the Penguins in the standings and appeared to be the better team. Led by Dale Hunter and a pesky Dino Ciccarelli, Washington had a high-powered offense that finished second in the league in goals scored. Their attack was well balanced as seven Capitals eclipsed the 20-goal plateau while 14 netted more than 10.

What's more, the Caps had defeated Pittsburgh five times in seven encounters during the regular season, a trend that continued through the first four games of the playoffs as Washington rolled to three easy victories and a commanding series lead.

One game away from elimination and down 2–1 with 12:07 remaining in the second period of Game Five, the Penguins fought back to win the contest, 5–2. Two nights later, Lemieux scored two goals and chipped in three assists to lead the Pens—who trailed by two goals at one point 4–2—to a 6–4 victory that set up a winner-take-all seventh and deciding game in Washington.

One of the biggest downfalls for the Pens in the regular season was a defense that was at times nonexistent, a characteristic that had been exploited by the high-scoring Capitals throughout the series. Pittsburgh had finished 20th in goals allowed in the 22-team National Hockey League, but for Game Seven, its defense would become its most valuable asset.

Odds were certainly against the Pens, since only 10 NHL teams had ever come back from a three-games-to-one deficit to win a playoff series, and of that small group, only one had triumphed on the road in Game Seven.

Washington had a chance to score early on a power play after Pittsburgh's Troy Loney was sent off for interference just over five minutes into the game. Instead, it was the Penguins who surged ahead when Ron Francis fired a shot past Capital goaltender Don Beaupre.

Washington tied the game in the second when Iafrate ripped a slap shot past Tom Barrasso, but it was apparent that Pittsburgh was playing a better defensive game, and it was only a matter of time before the Pens recaptured the lead. "We changed our style," Lemieux said later, "and played a very patient game."[1]

With 9:40 gone in the second period, Penguins second-year right winger Jaromir Jagr took a pass from Lemieux, then beating Beaupre with a shot to give the visitors an advantage they would not relinquish.

From then on, the Penguins' suddenly impenetrable defense repelled all of the Caps' scoring opportunities. They held the high-scoring Washington offense to only 19 shots in the game, including a mere eight in the third period when the Capitals were putting heavy pressure on Barrasso in an attempt to keep their season alive.

Finally, Pittsburgh right wing Joe Mullen tapped in an empty-net goal with only 33 seconds left on the clock to clinch the game and an improbable victory in the series.

"To make it to a seventh game and win tells you a lot about this team," coach Scotty Bowman said afterward. "We couldn't leave the season after losing in the fourth game."[2] The win did say a lot about the character of this team after the season they'd fought through. And their never-say-die attitude would serve them well in the weeks to come as they set out to defend their Stanley Cup title.

BOX SCORE

Teams	1	2	3	F
Pittsburgh	1	1	1	3
Washington	0	1	0	1

Per	Team	Goal (Assist)	Time
1	Pittsburgh	Lemieux 7 (Francis, Murphy)	14:01
2	Washington	Iafrate 4 (Ridley)	:24
2	Pittsburgh	Jagr 3 (Lemieux, Francis)	9:40
3	Pittsburgh	Mullen 3 (Francis)	19:27

Team	Goalie	Saves	Goals
Pittsburgh	Barrasso	18	1
Washington	Beaupre	18	2

Shots	1	2	3	T
Pittsburgh	7	8	6	21
Washington	6	5	8	19

#12

PENGUINS 10, PHILADELPHIA FLYERS 7
APRIL 25, 1989

The Rented Mule

One of the most popular of legendary Penguin announcer Mike Lange's many colorful sayings is "He beat him like a rented mule," which describes a player badly beating a goalie with a shot. When the Pittsburgh Penguins met the Philadelphia Flyers in Game Five of an Eastern Conference semifinal series in 1989, Philadelphia goalie Ron Hextall became the proverbial rented mule belonging to the Penguins . . . or more specifically to Mario Lemieux.

It had been a year that saw the Penguins finally start to turn the corner after six consecutive years of missing the playoffs. To complement Lemieux and some of the Pens' budding stars, in 1988 general manager Ed Johnston traded for Paul Coffey, arguably the greatest offensive defenseman in NHL history. Earlier in the 1988–89 campaign, Johnston's replacement, Tony Esposito, acquired goaltender Tom Barrasso from the Buffalo Sabres to give Pittsburgh the capable netminder that it had been looking for.

The new additions helped vault the Penguins to second place in the Patrick Division, falling only two points short of the franchise record. Offensively, the team had become one of the most dangerous in the league, while Lemieux surpassed Wayne Gretzky as the best player in the game. Lemieux had enjoyed a season for the ages, netting 85 goals while falling one point short of becoming only the second NHL player to eclipse the 200-point plateau. Robbie Brown was one of the most dangerous scorers in the league with 49 goals and 115 points, while Coffey became the third Pittsburgh player to garner 100 points during the season, chipping in 113.

Going into the playoffs with a newfound confidence, the Penguins won their first playoff series since 1979, sweeping the New York Rangers in the first round to set up their first-ever playoff matchup with their cross-state rivals, the

Philadelphia Flyers. The bad news for the upbeat Penguins was that the Flyers had spent the better part of their existence dominating Pittsburgh. Though the Pens finally ended their 15-year winless streak at the Spectrum earlier in the year and finished ahead of the Flyers in the standings, Philadelphia was still a tough, aggressive team and the Penguins knew they had to be at their best to survive the series.

The teams split the first four games, but the Flyers were winning the physical battle. Coffey had been slashed in a game, hurting his right thumb, while Lemieux had been the focus of the Flyers' attention defensively and had taken a beating. As the teams traveled to Pittsburgh for Game Five at the Civic Arena, Philadelphia was hoping to capitalize from the momentum of the 4–1 victory in Game Four, while the Pens hoped to prevent the Flyers from taking control of the series.

As it turned out, Lemieux and Co. had tolerated enough of the physical beating they'd been taking and quickly showed their opponents just how explosive they could be. Though he'd developed a sore neck earlier in the week, Lemieux started the game out on fire, setting the tone for a record-setting evening before the game was barely two minutes old.

He slapped a shot past Philly goalie Ron Hextall for his first goal of the game and then a minute and a half later notched his second. Before the game was seven minutes old, Lemieux had notched a natural hat trick (three consecutive goals) to give the Penguins a quick 3–0 lead. The flustered Hextall admitted afterward that this was "probably the best I've ever seen [Lemieux] play."[1]

It wasn't just Lemieux who was abusing Hextall. Twelve seconds later, Pittsburgh's Bob Errey scored his first goal of the series before former Penguin Mike Bullard put the Flyers on the board to make it 4–1. Lemieux then tied an NHL playoff record with his fourth goal of the period to restore the Pens' four-goal advantage. Teammate Troy Loney tacked on a score moments later, prompting Flyers coach Paul Holmgren to pull Hextall in favor of Ken Wregget with his team trailing, 6–1.

Philadelphia's Pelle Eklund set a league mark of his own as he scored the fastest playoff goal to start a period, six seconds in, cutting the lead back to four to give the Flyers a momentary lift. Hextall returned for the second period, but it was more of the same. Brown scored twice, and Kevin Stevens chipped another as the second period ended with the Penguins comfortably ahead, 9–3. After Brown's second goal, the irascible Hextall, sick of the beating he was taking as well as the intense taunting the Igloo fans were raining down on him, lost control and started to chase Brown. Hextall was given a 10-minute misconduct penalty, and it seemed Pittsburgh was cruising to an easy victory.

Unfortunately, the Flyers began to chip away at the lead in the third period, outshooting the Pens 21–7 and beating Barrasso four times to cut the seemingly insurmountable Pittsburgh advantage to only two goals with 2:37 remaining in regulation.

The once-raucous Civic Arena crowd had become subdued. A great victory was beginning to turn into the most incredible collapse in playoff history. Not surprisingly, Lemieux rode to the rescue, scoring an empty-net goal with less than a minute to play to secure a 10–7 victory and give the Penguins a three-to-two advantage in the series. His last goal put Lemieux in the record books once again, tying the all-time postseason marks for goals in a game with five, and points in one contest with eight.

While defeated, Philadelphia still had spirit, which, combined with frustration, led to an all-out melee on the ice with nine seconds left in the game, which resulted in 76 penalty minutes being doled out. The ruckus also set the tone for the final two games of the series, as the aggressive Flyers outscored the Penguins 10–3 to capture the series and leave a hungry Pittsburgh wondering what might have been.

Despite the disappointing outcome of the series, nothing could diminish the accomplishments of Lemieux and his teammates in Game Five. The frustrated face of Ron Hextall was all the proof necessary, that look of a rented mule that the Penguins had beaten time and time again.

BOX SCORE

Teams	1	2	3	F
Philadelphia	1	2	4	7
Pittsburgh	6	3	1	10

Per	Team	Goal (Assist)	Time
1	Pittsburgh	Lemieux 7 (Coffey, Stevens)	2:15
1	Pittsburgh	Lemieux 8 (Errey, Coffey)	3:45
1	Pittsburgh	Lemieux 9 (Cullen)	6:55
1	Pittsburgh	Errey 1 (Brown, Johnson)	7:07
1	Philadelphia	Bullard 2 (Ker, Samuelsson)	11:45
1	Pittsburgh	Lemieux 10 (Quinn)	17:09
1	Pittsburgh	Loney 1 (Johnson, Hannan)	17:44
2	Philadelphia	Eklund 2 (Kerr)	:06
2	Pittsburgh	Stevens 3 (Coffey, Lemieux)	1:43
2	Philadelphia	Propp 10 (Sutter, Chychrun)	9:07
2	Pittsburgh	Brown 4 (Lemieux, Zalapski)	10:35
2	Pittsburgh	Brown 5 (Lemieux, Coffey)	12:55
3	Philadelphia	Smith 1 (Carkner, Howe)	:48
3	Philadelphia	Kerr 11 (Secord, Acton)	10:21
3	Philadelphia	Eklund 3 (Propp, Murphy)	13:02
3	Philadelphia	Kerr 12 (Secord)	17:23
3	Pittsburgh	Lemieux 11 (Errey)	19:23

Team	Goalie	Saves	Goals
Philadelphia	Hextall	17	9
Philadelphia	Wregget	8	0
Pittsburgh	Barrasso	38	7

Shots	1	2	3	T
Philadelphia	9	15	21	45
Pittsburgh	18	10	7	35

#11

The Fergie Flyer

George Ferguson is a name only expert Pittsburgh Penguins fans would know. A center with the Penguins in the pre-championship era, Ferguson never garnered more than 53 points a year in his four-plus seasons in Pittsburgh, but he scored perhaps the single most dramatic goal in the franchise's first two decades.

After growing up in Trenton, Ontario, Ferguson was the first-round pick of the Toronto Maple Leafs in the 1972 entry draft, choosing to sign with the Maple Leafs over the World Hockey Association's Ottawa team, which also offered him a contract.

Though he never established himself as top-line forward, Ferguson none-theless tied an NHL playoff record when he scored three goals in one period against the Los Angeles Kings in 1978. Shortly after, Toronto traded Ferguson and defenseman Randy Carlyle to the Penguins for popular defenseman Dave Burrows.

The trade turned out to be very one-sided, with Pittsburgh getting the better end of the deal. After finishing with a substandard 25–37–18 mark in the 1977–78 campaign, Ferguson and Carlyle were perfect additions for a talented but young Pens squad. Greg Malone and Peter Lee both eclipsed the 30-goal plateau, while Ferguson led a group of four other players who each scored more than 20. The Penguins vaulted up the Norris Division standings, finishing in second place behind the Montreal Canadiens with a healthy 17-point improvement from the previous campaign.

The reward for their fine season was a trip to the playoffs and a first-round matchup with the Buffalo Sabres. After a slow start to the season, head coach Billy Inglis took over the reins of the Sabres and led them to an 88-point campaign, good enough for a second-place finish in the Adams Division. Though they finished with 17 fewer points than the previous season, the Sabres still played well enough to secure home-ice advantage over Pittsburgh.

While they had it, home ice proved to be no advantage at all as the visiting teams emerged victorious in the first two games of the best-of-three series. The Penguins captured the opening contest in Buffalo, 4–3, before the Sabres bounced back with a 3–1 victory in Game Two at the Civic Arena. The third and deciding contest would be played in front of a boisterous, sellout crowd at Buffalo's Memorial Auditorium.

The large throng enjoyed the early part of the game as the Sabres dominated play and outshot the Pens. Midway through the first period, Buffalo's Gilbert Perreault scored a power-play goal—the first either team had netted in 16 chances in this series—when he put back a rebound past Penguin goaltender Denis Herron to give Buffalo a 1–0 lead.

Before the roar from the jubilant home crowd could diminish, Pittsburgh left wing Jim Hamilton etched both his and Perreault's names in the record book when he scored five seconds later—an NHL playoff record for quickest consecutive goals.

Not to be outdone, Craig Ramsey restored Buffalo's lead, launching a scoring shot right before Pens defenseman Colin Campbell was about to hit him with a check to make it 2–1 three minutes later.

Buffalo took its lead into the second period along with the momentum, having outshot Pittsburgh 14–8 in the first 20 minutes. The Sabres appeared to be on the path to a series-ending victory when Hamilton, who'd been called up from the minors the day before, gave his team new life with his second goal of the game. Hamilton, who'd only scored two goals in 27 previous games with Pittsburgh, had matched that total in a 19-minute period.

Not wanting to disappoint the home crowd for a second time in this series, the Sabres rebounded when Buffalo defenseman Jerry Korab rifled a shot past Herron to end the second period with the Sabres again in the lead, 3–2.

With the momentum now reclaimed, the Sabres put incredible pressure on Herron in an effort to put the game and the series away. They outshot Pittsburgh 18–3 in the third, but Herron was impenetrable. While the Penguins only had three shots, they made the most of them. Buffalo goalie Bob Sauve turned aside a shot from Pittsburgh's Jacques Cossette, but Ferguson vaulted in and pushed the puck past Sauve to tie the score 3–3 with 16:43 remaining in regulation. Pittsburgh was able to survive the Sabres' pressure the rest of the period and, despite being outshot 40–23 on the evening, sent the game into overtime.

There have been many long overtime playoff games in the history of the Penguin franchise, but this was not one of them. One thing Ferguson was known for in his career was his speed, which had earned him the nickname the "Fergy Flyer." Just over 30 seconds into overtime, his trademark speed paid off. Skating briskly down the left side of the ice, Ferguson took in a perfect pass off the boards from Gregg Sheppard as he skated into the Sabres' end. Buffalo defenseman Mike Boland, who was chasing him, slipped as Ferguson zipped in on Sauve, and Ferguson slid the shot between the Buffalo goaltender's legs to win the game and the series.

"I knew Ferguson's speed would give him a [breakaway] chance," Pens broadcaster Mike Lange remembered. "The only question was whether he would score or not. He stuffed the puck in."[1]

Ferguson was also thrilled. "On the winning goal, I noticed the left side of the rink was open," he said. "I just took off, and when I thought I could score I just let it fly. I don't think it was anything different than I've been doing all season, but it sure meant a whole lot more."[2]

It certainly did. It was a goal that gave the Fergy Flyer a very important place in franchise history, scoring the game-winning goal in one of the young franchise's greatest victories.

BOX SCORE

Teams	1	2	3	OT	F
Pittsburgh	1	1	1	1	4
Buffalo	2	1	0	0	3

Per	Team	Goal (Assist)	Time
1	Buffalo	Perreault 1 (Martin, Robert)	12:59
1	Pittsburgh	Hamilton 1 (Sheppard)	13:04
1	Buffalo	Ramsay 1 (Luce, Seiling)	16:35
2	Pittsburgh	Hamilton 2 (Lee, Campbell)	11:47
2	Buffalo	Korab 1 (Dudley)	17:18
3	Pittsburgh	Ferguson 1 (Cossette, Blandon)	4:17
OT	Pittsburgh	Ferguson 2 (Sheppard, Carlyle)	:47

Team	Goalie	Saves	Goals
Pittsburgh	Herron	38	3
Buffalo	Sauve	20	4

Shots	1	2	3	OT	T
Pittsburgh	8	12	3	1	24
Buffalo	14	8	18	1	41

#10

The Kasparaitis Slide

On March 27, 1991, the Pittsburgh Penguins clinched the Patrick Division title with a 7–4 win over the Detroit Red Wings. That victory marked the Penguins' first title of any kind and the first of several championships the Penguins would capture over what would become the finest era in franchise history.

Nearly a quarter century of inept play was replaced by two Stanley Cup championships, five division titles, and 10 consecutive postseason appearances. But as the team began the 2000–2001 campaign, the 11th season since the beginning of its championship era, there were signs that the good times were coming to an end.

The main reason for the expected downturn was the precarious financial situation that the club was in. In order to remain solvent, new owner Mario Lemieux would not be able to keep the core of the team that had led the Penguins to such success. By 2003, stars such as Jaromir Jagr, Robert Lang, Alex Kovalev, and Darius Kasparaitis—a defenseman who was the heart and soul of the team—would be gone. But in 2001 they were still together and put together one final memorable season.

Pittsburgh finished third in the tough Atlantic Division, notching 96 points, and met the Southeast Division champion Washington Capitals in the first round of the playoffs. Though slight underdogs, the Pens disposed of the Capitals in a grinding six-game series in which five contests were decided by one goal.

The victory set up a conference semifinal matchup against the Buffalo Sabres. The Sabres had a very similar season to the Penguins, garnering only two more points than Pittsburgh, but had succeeded in a different way. While the Pens finished second in the league in scoring, Buffalo had the stingiest defense in the NHL, led by goaltender Dominik Hasek and his league-leading 2.11 goals against average.

Pittsburgh started off the series by winning the first two games in Buffalo and took what appeared to be a commanding lead in the series. The Sabres turned the tables at Mellon Arena with a pair of road victories to tie the series, then won Game Five in overtime back at Buffalo. With their backs against the wall, the Pens forced Game Seven with a dramatic 3–2 overtime victory in Pittsburgh.

A sellout crowd at HSBC Arena in Buffalo made for an intimidating atmosphere for the visitors, and the environment quickly got even worse when left wing J. P. Dumont beat Penguin goalie Johan Hedberg 1:50 into the second period to give the home team a 1–0 lead. Fitting with the back-and-forth nature of the series, Pittsburgh defenseman Andrew Ference silenced the crowd by netting a power-play goal six minutes later to tie the score.

With the score still knotted early in the third period, Buffalo took advantage of a high-sticking penalty on Lang and scored a power-play goal on a putback shot by right wing Steve Heinze to restore Buffalo's one-goal lead with under 20 minutes left to play.

As time ran down on both the game and—seemingly—the Penguins' championship era, Pittsburgh caught a break. Jagr fired a backhanded pass that deflected off former Penguin Stu Barnes, and the puck caromed to Lang, who put it past Hasek with 11 minutes remaining to make it 2–2. "It's a lucky goal," Hasek said later, "but my defenseman throws his stick. That's the reason they scored the goal."[1]

Still, Buffalo had a great opportunity to end the game and the series moments later, but Hedberg got his stick on the puck on a shot by a wide-open Vladimir Tsyplakov to keep the game tied.

The clock reached zero and the teams tumbled into overtime, where Pittsburgh dominated play with a 10–5 advantage in shots, most of which were excellent scoring chances. Still, the winning goal was something of a surprise.

Lang took the puck into the Buffalo zone with about seven minutes left in the extra session, passing it back to Kasparaitis, who had only three goals during the season, just 17 in his nine-year career, and only one in 54 postseason games. He sent a wrist shot past Hasek and into the net to win the game and send the Penguins to the Eastern Conference Finals. Kasparaitis celebrated by plopping down near center circle and sliding across the ice as his teammates dove on top of him.

One of the most surprised people in the building was Lemieux. "To be able to come out on top and have our sniper come through for us," he said, "was a great surprise, and we are all very excited. This is why I came back, to be able to be a part of the team and to live a dream, obviously. And hopefully we'll get to our dream, which is to win a Stanley Cup."[2]

The Penguins ultimately fell short of their dream, losing the conference championship to the New Jersey Devils in five games. But Game Seven of the Buffalo series shines brightly in the memories of Pittsburgh fans as the last great moment of the best era in team history—with the "Kasparaitis slide" serving as the lasting image of the Pens' final celebration.

BOX SCORE

Teams	1	2	3	OT	F
Pittsburgh	0	1	1	1	3
Buffalo	0	1	1	0	2

Per	Team	Goal (Assist)	Time
2	Buffalo	Dumont 4 (Barnes, Audette)	1:50
2	Pittsburgh	Ference 3 (Straka, Jagr)	8:19
3	Buffalo	Heinze 3 (Woolley, Gratton)	:32
3	Pittsburgh	Lang 3 (Straka, Jagr)	9:00
OT	Pittsburgh	Kaparaitis 1 (Lang, Jagr)	13:01

Team	Goalie	Saves	Goals
Pittsburgh	Hedberg	28	2
Buffalo	Hasek	25	3

Shots	1	2	3	OT	T
Pittsburgh	5	7	6	10	28
Buffalo	7	8	10	5	30

PENGUINS 4, NEW JERSEY DEVILS 3
APRIL 13, 1991

The Save

Stanley Cups are won through a long, painstaking process that consists of many different elements: building through the draft, making astute trades at the proper time, and great coaching, to name a few.

While it generally takes years to lay the groundwork for a championship, the inspiration for a title run can occur in a moment. Sometimes, without that one memorable moment to light the spark, careful and brilliant planning often falls short.

In the Pittsburgh Penguins' drive toward the 1991 Stanley Cup, that moment arrived in Game Six of the Patrick Division semifinal. Today, it's known simply as "The Save," one made by an unexpected hero.

Pittsburgh's Tom Barrasso was one of the premiere goaltenders in the league at the time, winning the Calder Trophy as the rookie of the year for the Buffalo Sabres in 1984 while also capturing the Vezina Trophy, given to the league's best netminder. By the time his career was over he would accumulate 369 wins, the 16th best mark in NHL history. As the Penguins were trailing the New Jersey Devils three games to two in their best-of-seven series and facing elimination, Barrasso was sidelined after a shoulder injury he suffered in Game Five.

With Pittsburgh's Stanley Cup hopes now on thin ice, coach Bob Johnson called on backup goalie Frank Pietrangelo to try and keep the season alive. The Ontario native had spent his first four seasons in the NHL as a second-string goalie for the Pens, the last three behind Barrasso. He had been solid if unspectacular, with his save percentage topping out at 89 percent.

Many doubted that he'd be able to stop the Devils in Game Six, but the 26-year-old goalie was excited about the opportunity. "Tom was hurt in Game

Five, and we knew that he would not be able to play the rest of the series," Pietrangelo said, "so I knew right away that I would be playing Game Six. As for what went through my mind, I was excited to get an opportunity to play on the 'big stage.'"[1]

Early in the contest it looked like neither Pietrangelo nor anyone else would be able to stop the Devils on their home ice, where the Penguins had lost six of their last seven games. Luck was on New Jersey's side at the 3:29 mark in the first period when John MacLean wristed a shot that bounced off Pittsburgh defenseman Larry Murphy past Pietrangelo for the game's opening goal.

Luckily, the 1990–91 Penguins had experience overcoming adversity all year, fighting through injuries to win the first division title in franchise history. They weren't about to fold now when the going got tough and allow such a special season come to an end. Pittsburgh left winger Kevin Stevens, who'd broken his nose in Game One, scored twice in less than three minutes to give Pittsburgh a 2–1 lead and silence the home crowd.

As the period was winding down, the Penguins were gaining confidence. Then came the moment that changed the course of franchise history.

With less than five minutes left in the first, Devils defenseman Viacheslav Fetisov launched a shot from the left point that was deflected by New Jersey's Brendan Shanahan. The puck veered to Pietrangelo's left as New Jersey sniper Peter Stastny skated in with hopes of slapping it into what appeared would be an empty net. Stastny, who would score 450 goals in his career, wristed the puck toward the net, apparently past Pietrangelo to tie the game. Shanahan raised his arms to celebrate, as did most of the crowd. But Pietrangelo quickly reached his glove hand out to catch the puck, robbing Stastny of a goal, and stun everyone who was watching.

Years later the backup netminder remembered the moment clearly. "The rebound went directly into the front of the crease," he said, "and there, all alone, was Peter Stastny with nothing but net in front of him. He fired the puck toward the open net, but somehow I just reached back, and the puck went into my catching glove. It was just a natural reaction for me, but it ended up being one of the great memories in Penguins history, and fortunately enough for me, I was involved."[2]

The save preserved the Pittsburgh lead, and things only got worse for the stunned Devils moments later. With 23 seconds left in the opening period, Jaromir Jagr buried a power-play goal to give Pittsburgh a two-goal advantage. Then the Penguins stretched the lead to three early in the second as newly acquired Ron Francis notched his second goal of the series to make the score 4–1.

The Pittsburgh defense—not at full strength with future Hall of Famer Paul

Coffey out with a scratched retina—was to be pressured by a strong New Jersey attack for the rest of the night, and Devils defensemen Eric Weinrich and Claude Lemieux scored within a minute of each other to cut the Penguin lead to a single goal late in the second period. Soon after that, the Devils appeared to have tied the game when Laurie Boschman beat Pietrangelo. But referee Bill McCreary waved off the goal, claiming that Boschman guided the puck past Pietrangelo with his skate. While the Pens' goalie said he clearly saw the puck being kicked in, Boschman disagreed. "It hit my skate and then my stick," he said. "It would have changed the momentum of the game completely, but what are you going to do?"[3]

The call swung momentum back on the Pens' side, and they shut down New Jersey the rest of the contest to hang on for a 4–3 victory that forced Game Seven in Pittsburgh. With Barrasso still out, Pietrangelo continued his storybook performance by shutting out the Devils 4–0 to clinch the series. While there would be many more great moments during this playoff run in 1991, there would be no more important one as the save against New Jersey that enabled the Penguins to win Game Six and stay alive in their quest toward the Stanley Cup title.

A moment that also etched Frank Pietrangelo's name in Pittsburgh sports history.

BOX SCORE

Teams	1	2	3	F
Pittsburgh	3	1	0	4
New Jersey	1	2	0	3

Per	Team	Goal (Assist)	Time
1	New Jersey	Maclean 5	3:29
1	Pittsburgh	Stevens 2 (Recchi)	10:49
1	Pittsburgh	Stevens 3 (Recchi, Mullen)	13:17
1	Pittsburgh	Jagr 2 (M. Lemieux, Francis)	19:37
2	Pittsburgh	Francis 3 (Recchi, Stevens)	6:42
2	New Jersey	Weinrich 1 (Driver, Shanahan)	12:32
2	New Jersey	C. Lemieux 4 (Ciger, Stastny)	13:48

Team	Goalie	Saves	Goals
Pittsburgh	Pietrangelo	28	3
New Jersey	Terreri	19	4

Shots	1	2	3	T
Pittsburgh	10	9	4	23
New Jersey	13	12	6	31

PENGUINS 5, NEW YORK RANGERS 4
MAY 9, 1992

When It Seems All Hope Is Gone

The Pittsburgh Penguins faced many trials and tribulations during the defense of their 1991 Stanley Cup championship. Not only did they face the usual challenges of a defending champion, but they had to overcome a huge emotional hurdle following the death of their head coach during the season. As tough as it had been, after rallying from a three-games-to-one deficit to defeat Washington in the first round of the playoffs, things would only get harder. In the division finals, the Penguins would meet the Patrick Division–champion New York Rangers, and the odds of Pittsburgh moving on to defend its cup victory began to dwindle.

After knocking off the Rangers 4–2 in the first contest at Madison Square Garden, Pittsburgh lost Game Two by the same score. And even worse, captain Mario Lemieux was knocked out of action with a fractured wrist after New York left wing Adam Graves inexplicably swung his stick at the Pens' star.

While Pittsburgh fans chastised Graves for what they perceived as dirty play, the Ranger left wing disagreed. "My intention wasn't to hurt [Lemieux], but I did hurt him," Graves recalled years later. "He's one of the great players to ever play, and as far as the game is concerned, those are the kinds of guys you want to see on the ice."[1]

Regardless of the intention, the league suspended Graves for four games, and Lemieux would be out for the rest of the series. Pittsburgh would undoubtedly miss Lemieux more than the Rangers would miss Graves.

Without their captain, the Penguins played inspired hockey but lost Game Three in overtime. With New York seemingly in control, a Rangers victory at the Civic Arena in Game Four would all but end the series and what had been a difficult year for the Pens.

As the season hung in the balance, things got off to a rough start for the home team. Former Penguin Randy Gilhen flipped a backhanded shot past Pittsburgh goalie Tom Barrasso to give New York a 1–0 lead before the game was five minutes old. Eight minutes later, New York's Tony Amonte increased the Ranger lead to two.

Pittsburgh's Mike Needham, who had never played an NHL game in the regular season at that point, scored his first career goal in only his second game to slow New York's momentum. Unfortunately, though, the Penguins became undisciplined in the middle of the second period. Rick Tocchet was sent off for slashing at the 9:51 mark and then Bob Errey went off for holding 22 seconds later, giving New York a two-man advantage for the better part of two minutes. New York's Mark Messier, who had sat out the previous two games with a torn muscle in his back, scored 36 seconds into the second penalty to make the score 3–1, Rangers. It appeared the battered Penguins were watching their season begin to circle the drain.

Just when it seemed like all hope was gone, the Pittsburgh Penguins remembered what it took to make them Stanley Cup champions the year before, and suddenly the series turned around.

With six seconds left in the period, Pittsburgh's Ron Francis scored on a power play, beating New York goalie Mike Richter and providing hope for the Penguins. Messier restored the Rangers' two-goal lead early in the third, but Francis rose to the occasion again. After Pittsburgh defenseman Gord Roberts was sent off for five minutes following a cross check, the Penguins killed the penalty by setting up a dramatic goal. Francis launched a long shot on Richter from outside the blue line, and the puck tipped off Richter's glove and into the goal, making the score 4–3. "I just lost sight of it, and it got in between my hip and glove," the Rangers' goalie said afterward. "When you've got the lead, you can't give them an inch, but that's what I gave them: an inch."[2]

Just over a minute later, Pittsburgh's Troy Loney beat Richter to tie the score, and the Civic Arena crowd was electrified, sensing a comeback victory in what had been a comeback season. Attempting to shift the momentum back New York's way, Rangers coach Roger Neilson replaced Richter with backup John Vanbiesbrouck.

Neither team was able to score for the rest of regulation, and the contest tumbled into sudden-death overtime. Only two minutes into the extra period, Pens right wing Jaromir Jagr drew a holding penalty on New York's Jeff Beukeboom, setting up a power play for the now resurgent Penguins. With time winding down in the one-man advantage, Pittsburgh defenseman Larry Murphy stole the puck from Messier and fired a shot toward the net. Francis took the rebound and sent the puck past Vanbiesbrouck for the winning goal—his third of the game—to send the sellout throng into hysterics.

The goal not only won the game and tied the series but seemed to signify the moment when the Penguins finally realized they were still the best team in the league. From that night on, they didn't lose another game in the postseason, rattling off 10 consecutive victories on their way to capturing a second straight championship—one that many Pittsburgh fans had abandoned any hopes of achieving before their fateful Game Four victory over New York.

BOX SCORE

Teams	1	2	3	OT	F
New York	2	1	1	0	4
Pittsburgh	1	1	2	1	5

Per	Team	Goal (Assist)	Time
1	New York	Gilhen 1	4:56
1	New York	Amonte 3 (Gartner)	13:04
1	Pittsburgh	Needham 1 (Loney, Callander)	13:28
2	New York	Messier 6 (Leetch, Gartner)	10:49
2	Pittsburgh	Francis 4 (Stevens, Stanton)	19:54
3	New York	Messier 7 (Amonte, Beukeboom)	:46
3	Pittsburgh	Francis 5 (Hrdina, Stevens)	10:27
3	Pittsburgh	Loney 3 (Jagr, Murphy)	11:52
OT	Pittsburgh	Francis 6 (Murphy, Stevens)	2:47

Team	Goalie	Saves	Goals
New York	Richter	21	4
New York	Vanbiesbrouck	10	1
Pittsburgh	Barrasso	26	4

Shots	1	2	3	OT	T
New York	13	8	9	0	30
Pittsburgh	6	13	13	4	36

#7

PENGUINS 5, CHICAGO BLACK HAWKS 4
MAY 26, 1992

Never Let Him Out of Your Sight

Mike Keenan was a tough, brilliant coach who always seemed to get the best out of his players. In eight seasons leading the Philadelphia Flyers and Chicago Blackhawks, he won three conference championships. The only goal at the time Keenan hadn't achieved in his fine career was winning a Stanley Cup, falling short in the finals twice with the Flyers in the mid-1980s. He'd have another chance in 1992 when he guided Chicago to the finals against Jaromir Jagr, Mario Lemieux, and the defending-champion Pittsburgh Penguins.

Like the Pens, as they endured a difficult follow-up season, Chicago struggled throughout 1991–92. Still, led by 50-goal scorer Jeremy Roenick and goaltender Ed Belfour, the Blackhawks notched a respectable 87 points and finished second in their division behind the Detroit Red Wings.

Keenan had his team ready by the time the postseason started, though, as the Blackhawks quickly got on a roll. They won three straight games to rally from behind in their first-round series with St. Louis and then stunned the heavily favored Red Wings with a four-game sweep. In the Campbell Conference Finals, Chicago made quick work of the Edmonton Oilers with another sweep, extending their postseason win streak to 11 games.

Once again, Keenan had demonstrated his brilliance as a coach, but by the end of Game One of the Stanley Cup Finals, it appeared Keenan had forgotten to underline one important strategy for any team facing the Pens: you always need to keep an eye on Mario Lemieux.

Just like the Blackhawks, the Penguins had caught fire in the postseason. After struggling against Washington in the first round and falling behind New York in the conference semifinals, the Penguins found their stride, winning the last three against New York and then sweeping the Boston Bruins in the

Wales Conference Finals. Even though they weren't necessarily the best two teams during the regular season, the hottest teams in hockey would take the ice at the Civic Arena for Game One.

For the first half of the contest, it appeared as though Chicago would cruise to victory. Chicago defenseman Chris Chelios opened up the scoring at 6:34 of the first period with a power-play goal to give the Blackhawks a 1–0 lead. Michel Goulet then notched his third goal of the postseason to increase Chicago's lead to two before Dirk Graham beat Tom Barrasso 26 seconds later, giving the visitors a 3–0 advantage.

Pittsburgh's Phil Bourque closed Chicago's lead to two goals with a power-play goal of his own late in the first, but midway in the second, Blackhawk Steve Larmer found Brent Sutter with a perfect pass that set up the 29-year-old center to score Chicago's fourth goal and give the Blackhawks what seemed like an insurmountable 4–1 lead. It had been 48 years since a team blew a three-goal lead in a game in the Stanley Cup Finals—though, ironically, that team had been the 1944 Chicago Blackhawks, as history was about to repeat itself.

With under five minutes remaining in the second period, Pittsburgh's Rich Tocchet began the comeback when he beat Belfour to make the score 4–2. Less than a minute later, Lemieux made it a one-goal contest with his 12th postseason score. The Pens were now firmly back in the game as it entered the third period.

Chicago had been rocked on its heels, but Belfour rose to the occasion in the third period, and it seemed like the Blackhawks would be able to hold on for the victory. Unfortunately for Chicago fans, with just under five minutes left in the game, Jagr showed why he was on the brink of becoming one of the most exciting players in hockey. After taking the puck at the boards to the right of the Chicago goalie, he skated around Sutter and turned defenseman Frantisek Kucera around before going past Igor Kravchuk and flipping a backhand shot to the right of Belfour, who appeared to have not seen the shot. Jagr's amazing play had brought the Penguins all the way back to tie the game.

The contest appeared to be headed for overtime as the teams lined up for a face-off to the left of Belfour with less than 20 seconds remaining in regulation and the Penguins with a one-man advantage. Pittsburgh's Ron Francis won the face-off, sending the puck back to defenseman Larry Murphy, who rifled a slap shot at the Blackhawk goalie. Belfour turned it aside, but none of the Blackhawks had kept an eye on Lemieux, who hustled toward the goal and lifted the puck into the open net to give Pittsburgh its first lead of the game with only 13 seconds left. The score allowed the Pens to win a game they probably should have lost.

Keenan was distraught after the game. "To give up a three-goal lead in the Stanley Cup Finals is inexcusable," he said. "We made mistakes we haven't made the whole playoffs. There's no excuse for it."[1]

Just as there was no excuse for not keeping tabs on hockey's best player with the game on the line.

BOX SCORE

Teams	1	2	3	F
Chicago	3	1	0	4
Pittsburgh	1	2	2	5

Per	Team	Goal (Assist)	Time
1	Chicago	Chelios 6 (Sutter)	6:34
1	Chicago	Goulet 3	13:17
1	Chicago	Graham 4 (Chelios)	13:43
1	Pittsburgh	Bourque 3 (Tocchet, Francis)	17:26
2	Chicago	Sutter 3 (Larmer, Chelios)	11:36
2	Pittsburgh	Tocchet 5 (Stanton, McEachern)	15:24
2	Pittsburgh	Lemieux 12 (Stevens)	16:23
3	Pittsburgh	Jagr 10	15:05
3	Pittsburgh	Lemieux 13 (Francis, Murphy)	19:47

Team	Goalie	Saves	Goals
Chicago	Belfour	34	5
Pittsburgh	Barrasso	30	4

Shots	1	2	3	T
Chicago	11	11	12	34
Pittsburgh	15	10	14	39

PENGUINS 8, NEW JERSEY DEVILS 6
DECEMBER 31, 1988

Five Goals, Five Ways

There are five possible scenarios in which you can score a goal in the game of hockey: even strength, on the power play, shorthanded, on a penalty shot, and into an empty net. While all are fairly common, in the first 71 years of the NHL's existence, no player had ever scored a goal through each method in a single game. On New Year's Eve 1988, that changed when one of the greatest players in NHL history achieved perhaps his most amazing feat.

By the time 1988 had come around, the greatness that many had predicted for the 23-year-old Mario Lemieux was beginning to come to fruition. He led the league in both goals and points scored the year before with 70 and 168 respectively, capturing the first of what would be three MVP awards. As he came into the final contest of the 1988 calendar year, he was closing in on his 100th point, hoping to become only the second player in league history to reach the plateau so quickly (Wayne Gretzky had done it twice). It was an achievement he would match in a most spectacular way against an opponent the Penguins generally struggled with.

The New Jersey Devils had dominated the Pens over their previous seven meetings, winning five and tying two. It seemed like things would be different this time around since Pittsburgh was challenging for the division lead and the Devils were simply trying to keep out of the division cellar. To make matters worse for New Jersey, the Devils came into the game without leading scorer John MacLean and starting goaltender Sean Burke.

New Jersey coach Jim Schoenfeld called on backup Bob Sauve, a former Penguin, to face Pittsburgh at the Civic Arena in the hopes of ringing in the New Year by continuing their unbeaten streak against the Pens.

Despite the individual stardom that would be displayed that night, it was a tight game. The Devils started out strong when left wing Jim Korn beat Pens goalie Tom Barrasso 3:39 into the game for a 1–0 New Jersey lead, but 38 seconds later, Lemieux began his memorable performance scoring a goal under the most common circumstances, with the teams at even strength. Breaking toward the New Jersey goal, the Pens' captain passed the puck in front of the net toward teammate Bob Errey, but the puck glanced off New Jersey defenseman Craig Wolanin and went past Sauve into the goal to tie the contest.

His second goal was classic Mario. With the Penguins shorthanded, Lemieux took a pass from defenseman Randy Hillier and skated between two Devils. He then pulled the puck around center Aaron Broten before sliding the backhander past a prone Sauve. It was 2–1 Pens, and Lemieux was just getting warmed up.

New Jersey's Kirk Mueller tied the game moments later, but the lead was only temporary as Lemieux would complete his first-period hat trick while the Devils were a man down. Taking a pass from Paul Coffey, Lemieux launched a slap shot from the face-off circle past the beaten netminder to give the Pens a 3–2 advantage that they would hold on to as the opening period came to an end.

The scoring spree continued through the first eight minutes of the second period as the Devils and Penguins exchanged two goals apiece. Pittsburgh's Robbie Brown started things off, giving the Pens a two-goal advantage 39 seconds into the period. Lemieux was credited with an assist on the goal, giving him his first milestone of the day with his 100th point in only his 38th game, the third fastest to that tally in league history. New Jersey's Tommy Albelin cut the margin to 4–3 before Pittsburgh's Dan Quinn notched his 18th to extend the lead again. Mueller scored his second of the contest 48 seconds later to pull New Jersey back to within a goal, setting up the most exciting and difficult goal in Lemieux's attempt at history.

With 8:46 left in the period, referee Dan Maourelli awarded Lemieux a penalty shot after goalie Chris Terreri, who replaced Sauve after Quinn's goal, threw his stick at Lemieux in a desperate attempt to stop him from scoring again. Lemieux, two for two in his career in penalty shots, slid the puck between Terreri's legs for his fourth goal of the game and a 6–4 lead.

Ironically, for Lemieux to complete the improbable feat, the Devils would have to remain close enough to the Penguins to justify pulling their goalie in the final moments. After the teams traded goals to make the score 7–5, the Devils' Anders Carlsson tallied his second goal of the season with 3:36 left in the game to set up the empty-net situation Lemieux needed.

Time proved to be the biggest obstacle, and the clock ticked toward zero without out Lemieux getting a chance to score. With only five seconds left, Jay Caufield hit Lemieux with a pass inside the Devils' zone, and he quickly put the puck into the empty net with one second remaining to complete the incredible—and unlikely—feat.

The Pens' captain had set a team record with five goals and tied his own mark with eight points as he had a hand in all of the Penguin goals, but those marks, as well as his 100-point achievement, were overshadowed. What endures today is the five different ways he scored and that he remains the only player in league history to accomplish it in a single game.

BOX SCORE

Teams	1	2	3	F
New Jersey	2	3	1	6
Pittsburgh	3	4	1	8

Per	Team	Goal (Assist)	Time
1	New Jersey	Korn 8 (Mueller, Kurvers)	3:39
1	Pittsburgh	Lemieux 39 (R. Brown)	4:17
1	Pittsburgh	Lemieux 40 (Hillier)	7:50
1	New Jersey	Mueller 12 (Verbeek, Korn)	9:46
1	Pittsburgh	Lemieux 41 (Coffey, Dineen)	10:59
2	Pittsburgh	R. Brown 27 (Quinn, Lemieux)	:39
2	New Jersey	Albelin 4 (D. Brown, Carlsson)	5:14
2	Pittsburgh	Quinn 18 (R. Brown, Lemieux)	7:39
2	New Jersey	Mueller 13 (Cichocki, Albelin)	8:27
2	Pittsburgh	Lemieux 42 Penalty Shot	11:14
2	New Jersey	Kurvers 11 (Mueller, Korn)	11:43
2	Pittsburgh	Bourque 13 (R. Brown, Lemieux)	16:35
3	New Jersey	Carlsson 2 (Mueller, Anderson)	16:24
3	Pittsburgh	Lemieux 43 (Caufield)	19:59

Team	Goalie	Saves	Goals
New Jersey	Sauve	5	5
New Jersey	Terreri	6	2
Pittsburgh	Barrasso	29	6

Shots	1	2	3	T
New Jersey	11	10	14	35
Pittsburgh	8	6	5	19

Sweeter the Second Time Around

Not everything is better the second time around, but as the Pittsburgh Penguins closed in on a second straight Stanley Cup championship in 1992, it was even sweeter than the year before. Overcoming so many obstacles over the course of a tumultuous season had made the team truly appreciate what they had accomplished—and were about to accomplish.

After stumbling through the season and the early part of the playoffs, the Penguins got on a roll that continued through a tough physical series in the Stanley Cup Finals against the Campbell Conference–champion Chicago Blackhawks. While each of the first three games had been close, the Penguins had found a way to win each and now stood at the brink of a four-game sweep.

Only twice in the history of major professional sports in North America at that time had a team come back from such a deficit, and one of those occasions had seen the Penguins squandering a three-game lead. Still, the odds were against Chicago capturing its first cup since 1960, and coach Mike Keenan knew he would have to come up with a drastic change in strategy if he was going to keep the season alive. His maneuver was to go away from his physical defensive style in favor of a wide-open offensive attack. It was a bold move, but one that better fit the Penguins' style of play.

The maneuver took the Penguins by surprise and resulted in a wild first period of Game Four at Chicago Stadium. The tone was set early when Chicago goaltender Ed Belfour tried unsuccessfully to clear the puck from behind his net, and instead gave it to the Pens' Jaromir Jagr, who circled in front of the cage and beat the Blackhawk goalie 1:37 into the contest.

As they would continue to do throughout the game, Chicago stormed back. Stephane Matteau fed Dirk Graham right in front of Pittsburgh goalie Tom

Barrasso, who stopped Graham's backhand attempt, but then Graham poked the rebound past the fallen netminder to tie the score.

Intrigued by Keenan's strategy, the Penguins wanted to show the Blackhawks they'd made a mistake. Twelve seconds after Chicago tied it, Lemieux fed Stevens to the left of Belfour. With former Penguin defenseman Rod Buskas hanging on him, Stevens sent a soft backhand shot past Belfour to give Pittsburgh a 2–1 lead. With no margin for error, Keenan pulled Belfour in favor of rookie goalie Dominik Hasek.

It took Chicago only 18 seconds to respond this time, with Graham's second goal of the game to make it 2–2 and give Chicago new life. While Hasek would soon become one of the best goalies in the game, he wasn't there quite yet. After Hasek made a nice stop of a slap shot from Pittsburgh defenseman Larry Murphy at the point, Lemieux took the rebound and sent it into the open net for a 3–2 Penguin lead. But once again, Chicago answered just before the first period closed when right wing Brian Noonan sent a pass through the goal mouth past Barrasso and onto the stick of Graham, who completed his hat trick to tie the game at three.

Just like they had in the first, the Penguins scored very quickly in the second. Stevens took the puck behind Hasek and fed a wide-open Rick Tocchet, who scored 58 seconds into the period to give Pittsburgh back the lead at 4–3. Still not succumbing to another momentum shift, Chicago tied the game one last time late in the period when Jeremy Roenick notched his 11th goal of the playoffs heading into the final period.

After two periods the Blackhawks' new strategy seemed to be working just fine. But they were about to discover it was difficult to keep up with the Penguins' talent for a full game. "If they want to play us like that," Barrasso said afterward, "we're going to score more goals than them running and gunning any night of the week."[1]

Pittsburgh put incredible pressure on Hasek early in the third. The Blackhawk backup goalie hung tough, stopping Lemieux on a breakaway, then saw a slap shot from Murphy just miss. Finally Murphy wristed one past Hasek to give the Pens a lead they would not relinquish.

Three minutes after Murphy put Pittsburgh in front, Pittsburgh center Ron Francis skated in on a two-on-one break with Shawn McEachern. Francis leaned as if he were going to pass to McEachern, then ripped a slap shot that beat Hasek to his short side, giving Pittsburgh a 6–4 lead with 12 minutes left.

Now playing with a sense of desperation, Chicago did not go quietly. Roenick beat Barrasso a second time to bring the Blackhawks to within one, and with time running out, Chicago continued to put pressure on the Pens' goalie. They had one final chance to extend the series with seconds left when defenseman Chris Chelios launched a shot at Barrasso, which was blocked as the horn sounded.

Barrasso danced in his crease as his teammates mobbed him. Pens announcer Mike Lange screamed to his audience, "Lord Stanley, Lord Stanley, give me the brandy!"[2] The Penguins took turns parading around the ice hoisting the famed trophy that only a month ago seemed unattainable.

Keenan made no excuses for his team's play as it became the 16th team to be swept in the Stanley Cup Finals. "They've got a collection of great players," he said of the Penguins. "We were just beaten by a better club. They have youth, experience, and the greatest player in the world."[3]

As Lemieux, the greatest player in the world in Keenan's (and others') opinion, got his turn with the cup, it was announced that he also won his second consecutive Conn Smythe Award as the MVP of the playoffs.

The victory was joyous, but also reflective, as the players took time to think about everything it took to get to this point—and the man who helped take them there, who was no longer with them. To honor their late coach Bob Johnson, the league allowed the franchise to have his named etched on the Stanley Cup.

It was an appropriate way to celebrate a repeat championship that was even sweeter than the first.

BOX SCORE

Teams	1	2	3	F
Pittsburgh	3	1	2	6
Chicago	3	1	1	5

Per	Team	Goal (Assist)	Time
1	Pittsburgh	Jagr 11 (Loney)	1:37
1	Chicago	Graham 5 (Matteau, Chelios)	6:21
1	Pittsburgh	Stevens 13 (M. Lemieux, Tocchet)	6:33
1	Chicago	Graham 6 (Chelios)	6:51
1	Pittsburgh	M. Lemieux 16 (Murphy, Stevens)	10:13
1	Chicago	Graham 7 (Noonan, J. Lemieux)	16:16
2	Pittsburgh	Tocchet 6 (M. Lemieux, Stevens)	:58
2	Chicago	Roenick 11 (Noonan, Gilbert)	15:40
3	Pittsburgh	Murphy 6 (Tocchet)	4:51
3	Pittsburgh	Francis 8 (McEachern, Paek)	7:59
3	Chicago	Roenick 12 (Grimson, Buskas)	11:18

Team	Goalie	Saves	Goals
Pittsburgh	Barrasso	24	5
Chicago	Belfour	2	2
Chicago	Hasek	21	4

Shots	1	2	3	T
Pittsburgh	12	9	8	29
Chicago	8	14	7	29

Spit Shine Your Shoes

In the fall of 1974, Mike Lange was hired as a broadcaster for the Pittsburgh Penguins, beginning a long career that would eventually turn him into a Steel City institution. Except for one season, the 1975–76 campaign when he left the team for one season after it declared bankruptcy, Lange was a constant with the franchise, making a name for himself for his colorful and peculiar sayings during a game. Little gems like "Michael, Michael motorcycle," "He beat him like a rented mule," "Buy Sam a drink and get his dog one too," and "She wants to sell my monkey"[1] have become legendary to loyal Penguin fans young and old. But the one call he hadn't gotten to make in his first 16 seasons behind the mike with the Penguins was one proclaiming a championship.

While the Penguins captured their first division title in 1991, it wasn't quite at the level to warrant a memorable on-air moment. Fans wondered what memorable saying he would concoct if Pittsburgh were crowned a conference champion. When the club faced the Boston Bruins at the Civic Arena for Game Six of the Wales Conference Finals, Penguins fans hoped by the evening's end that Lange would have the chance to say something that would be long remembered by the Penguin nation.

Not that a Penguins victory was assured. The Bruins were led by 30-year-old superstar defenseman Ray Bourque, who was trying to win his first Stanley Cup, and 50-goal scorer Cam Neely, who broke the plateau for the second consecutive season. Boston had triumphed in the first two games of the series at Boston Garden before the series changed gears on one memorable hit in Game Three in Pittsburgh. Pens defenseman Ulf Samuelsson, widely accused of being one of the dirtiest players in the league, took Neely out on a nasty knee-to-knee hit. Neely continued to play, but both he and the Bruins offense weren't the same. Pittsburgh outscored Boston 15–4 in three straight victories to take a three-games-to-two lead in the series, putting them one game away from reaching their first Stanley Cup Finals.

The sellout crowd of 16,164 was on hand in anticipation of seeing Penguins history being made as the two teams took the Civic Arena ice for Game Six. But the Bruins were committed to preventing that from happening as they took an early 1–0 lead on a power-play goal by Neely. Two minutes later, Boston's Ken Hodge increased the cushion to two goals with a power-play goal of his own after the Pens were whistled for too many men on the ice.

The fans who'd shown up expecting a party were stunned. They'd be reminded that other than Lange, the other constant in Penguin history was playoff failure and disappointment, and it looked like it might happen once again.

But this Penguin team wasn't about to allow that history to repeat itself. Mario Lemieux took the puck to the right of Bruin goalie Andy Moog and wound up for a slap shot right outside the face-off circle, but then he saw defenseman Larry Murphy open and fired a quick pass to him. Murphy wristed it past Moog to cut the Boston lead to 2–1.

Now invigorated, the Penguins took the puck into the Bruins' zone as time was running out in the second period. Mark Recchi skated with the puck behind the net and around to the front before taking a shot that Moog stopped. The rebound came out to Phil Bourque, who, seconds before, had been knocked to the ice. He leaped to his feet, grabbed the rebound, and flipped the puck above Moog, tying the game and sending the once-quiet crowd into hysterics. As the third period began, Recchi fed defenseman Gord Roberts for a goal to put the Penguins ahead.

But just when it seemed Pittsburgh had control, the Bruins once again silenced the Civic Arena crowd when Boston's Don Sweeney put back a rebound to tie the game with less than eight minutes left in regulation.

With overtime looming, Recchi once again made a spectacular play. The Bruins were aggressively forechecking the Pens in their own end as Roberts launched a cross-ice pass that found Recchi skating in toward Moog. The Wrecking Ball, as Lange often called Recchi during broadcasts, ripped a shot past the Boston goaltender for the lead that Pittsburgh would not relinquish as only 4:20 remained in the game.

Lemieux added an empty-net goal with 28 seconds remaining to clinch the victory, and as the crowd counted down the final seconds, fans listening on the radio leaned forward to hear Lange's long-awaited championship call. As the clock struck zero, the Penguin broadcaster proclaimed, "You can spit shine your shoes, cause the Pens are going dancing with Lord Stanley!"

Other exciting times were ahead for this young squad in the coming weeks, but for now, after 24 tortuous seasons, they could celebrate the biggest moment in the franchise's history—the night in which, as Lange had said, they'd finally landed a date to dance with Lord Stanley.

BOX SCORE

Teams	1	2	3	F
Boston	0	2	1	3
Pittsburgh	0	2	3	5

Per	Team	Goal (Assist)	Time
2	Boston	Neely 16 (Wiemer, R. Bourque)	7:16
2	Boston	Hodge 4 (R. Bourque, B. Sweeney)	9:33
2	Pittsburgh	Murphy 4 (Lemieux, Young)	11:45
2	Pittsburgh	P. Bourque 4 (Murphy, Recchi)	17:17
3	Pittsburgh	Roberts 1 (Recchi, Lemieux)	10:08
3	Boston	D. Sweeney 3 (Christian, Lazaro)	12:13
3	Pittsburgh	Recchi 8 (Roberts)	15:40
3	Pittsburgh	Lemieux 11	19:32

Team	Goalie	Saves	Goals
Boston	Moog	23	4
Pittsburgh	Barrasso	25	3

Shots	1	2	3	T
Boston	7	11	10	28
Pittsburgh	7	7	14	28

On the Road Again

The success of the professional teams that call the Steel City home has been well documented. The Penguins were on the verge of winning their fourth Stanley Cup championship; the Steelers have won more Super Bowls than any other NFL franchise; and the Pittsburgh Pirates count five World Series trophies in their illustrious history. Add to the mix Pitt football's nine national championships and Duquesne University's basketball national championship in 1955 and it becomes remarkable to think that it had been 56 years since a Pittsburgh team in a major sport had won a championship on Pittsburgh soil.

Many will point out the Pittsburgh Triangles took the World Team Tennis championship at home in 1975, while the Pittsburgh Hornets of the AHL and the ABA's Pittsburgh Pipers won titles in Pittsburgh in 1967 and 1968, respectively. Each is true, but those weren't considered major leagues at the time. When it comes to the four major leagues in the United States—the MLB, NHL, NFL and NBA—Bill Mazeroski's majestic homerun in the bottom of the ninth inning of the seventh game at Forbes Field to defeat the New York Yankees in the 1960 World Series, was the last time a Pittsburgh team raised a trophy on home soil. In fact, before the Pittsburgh Penguins took on the San Jose Sharks in the fifth game of the 2016 Stanley Cup Finals with a chance to end the series in Pittsburgh, Steel City clubs in the four major leagues had captured 14 championships with only two won in Pittsburgh (the other being the 1925 World Series when Kiki Cuyler smashed a two-run double in the bottom of the eighth to win the title 9–7 once again at Forbes Field).

Having the chance to break the streak was something the entire town embraced enthusiastically. The Pens invited Mazeroski to the Consol Center in hopes he could relive his magical moment by watching the team hoist the cup. The tickets for the event were being sold on the online ticket outlets for upwards of $10,000. There was a sellout crowd at the arena with so many people lining the streets outside the Consol Center to watch the game on the big screen TV that the city quickly had to arrange for another TV to be placed in the Market Square area to handle the overflow crowd.

The city was ready to erupt with the fans certain of a victory. The only problem was that the Penguins actually had to play the game against a San Jose team that pushed them to the limit in each contest of the series.

To the disappointment of the many that descended on Pittsburgh on this warm June evening, the Sharks played their best game in the finals, taking a quick 2–0 lead. After allowing the Pens to tie it up, they retook control for the 4–2 victory. The city was devastated. Not only would their beloved team have to travel to the Bay Area for a sixth game, but if the team lost, it would return here in a different light, with the momentum firmly on the side of the Sharks, the team that many experts placed as favorites before the finals began. Tradition seemed to dictate that a Pittsburgh team was destined to win a title on the road, and as the great Willie Nelson said in his famous song, the Penguins were now on the road again.

Seven years to the day that the franchise won its last Stanley Cup title—on the road in Detroit where they defeated the Red Wings 2–1 in 2009—Pittsburgh would once again have the opportunity to win a title away from home. They would have to do so in front of a loud aggressive crowd who was enjoying the fruits of their first Western Conference championship in the 25th year of their existence.

Except for a less-than-stellar performance in the previous matchup, Pittsburgh had dominated play in the series, and they had to reestablish that domination if they hoped to win in this hostile atmosphere. San Jose, however, would try to continue their efforts from Game Five. It was apparent early on that Pittsburgh would be the ones who were in control.

Captain Sidney Crosby made a statement from the beginning that the Pens were coming out aggressively in this game, slashing Joe Thornton on the opening face-off. The team went on to outshoot the Sharks 9–4 in the first as defenseman Brian Dumoulin gave the Pens an early one-goal lead after San Jose's Dainius Zubrus was sent off for tripping. He took a pass from Justin Schultz and then faked a shot against the Sharks' Melker Karlsson, which gave him an open shot from the point against goalie Martin Jones. He beat him on the slap shot for the 1–0 advantage.

After a video tribute on the scoreboard honoring the great Gordie Howe, who passed away just two days earlier, the second period began with San Jose finally getting some opportunities against Matt Murray. After a turnover right outside their zone, Brent Burns knocked down the puck and found the leading scorer in the playoffs, Logan Couture, who beat Murray for his 10th goal and 30th point in the postseason becoming the fourth player since 1996 to garner 30 or more points in the playoffs (Evgeni Malkin and Crosby both turned the trick in 2009).

With the score tied at one and the crowd in San Jose as loud as they could be, thoughts that a Game Seven would occur seemed very realistic. As they had done so many times in the previous rounds, Pittsburgh responded quickly. Crosby took the puck behind the net and flipped it to Kris Letang. Letang was at a bad angle and sent a shot toward Jones. Fortunately, it hit off the San Jose goaltender and tricked between his legs to put the Pens back up front by a goal only 1:19 after the Sharks seemingly had taken the momentum. While the game remained close the rest of the way, it was only a facade, as the Penguins dominated play.

Pittsburgh had many opportunities that Jones turned away after the Letang goal, including a two-on-one break with Malkin and Chris Kunitz where Malkin passed the puck to Kunitz who had a wide open net in front of him. Inexplicably, instead of shooting, he passed the puck back to Malkin who was too far in toward the goal to take a meaningful shot.

As the two teams entered the rink for the third period, the fact remained that San Jose was one shot away from tying the game; unfortunately for the home crowd, the Pens' tight defense would play almost perfectly. They stunted the Shark offense in the final period with aggressive forechecking and blocking shots when needed. The Pens allowed San Jose only one shot on Murray before Crosby blocked a pass with a little over a minute remaining. The puck deflected perfectly to Patric Hornqvist. Hornqvist rushed it up the ice and flicked the puck into the open net at 18:58 to put the game out of reach.

Putting a harmless second shot on goal was all the Sharks could muster in the final 1:02 as Pittsburgh held on for the 3–1 victory and with it their fourth Stanley Cup. The team was euphoric as Crosby, the Conn Smythe Award winner symbolic of the postseason MVP, took the Stanley Cup for the second time in his career, parading it around the ice before handing it over to Trevor Daley, whose mother was suffering from cancer and wanted to see her son hoist it on national TV. Daley gave it to Pascal Dupuis, who had retired earlier in the season because of a blood clot condition, who then turned it over to the team's regular season MVP Marc-Andre Fleury, who played only twice in the postseason after suffering his second concussion late in the regular campaign. After that the rest of the team got their opportunities with the cup, celebrating what had been a stunning season that started so poorly.

Pittsburgh teams had become accustomed to winning championships on the road. While Steel City fans once again were not given the opportunity to witness championships they did not feel cheated. Many roamed on the city's South Side following the contest, and a record 400,000 came to the city to see their road warriors in the traditional championship parade. Winning a title on the road is not a sore spot for the citizens of this fine city—it's a treasured Pittsburgh tradition.

BOX SCORE

Team	1	2	3	F
Pittsburgh	1	1	1	3
San Jose	0	1	0	1

Per	Team	Goal (Assist)	Time
1	Pittsburgh	Dumoulin 2 (Schultz, Kunitz) PP	8:16
2	San Jose	Couture 10 (Karlsson, Burns)	6:27
2	Pittsburgh	Letang 3 (Crosby, Sheary)	7:46
3	Pittsburgh	Hornqvist 9 (Crosby) EN	18:58

Team	Goalie	Saves	Goals
Pittsburgh	Murray	18	1
San Jose	Jones	24	2

Shots	1	2	3	T
Pittsburgh	9	11	7	27
San Jose	4	13	2	19

A Dream Come True

Pittsburgh sports fans of the twenty-first century begin nearly every hockey season almost assured that the Penguins not only will make the postseason but will be one of the favorites to win the Stanley Cup. Four decades earlier, when the franchise was in its infancy, it was a much different time.

As the Penguins were just getting started in the 1970s, all the talk in Pittsburgh centered around the Pirates (who won six division titles and a pair of World Series in the decade) and the Steelers (seven division titles and four Super Bowl championships). Meanwhile, the Pens were simply trying to keep out of last place, hoping to overcome their financial woes so they could remain in Pittsburgh. In their first 24 seasons, they'd reached the playoffs a modest 10 times and finished with a total of six winning records.

This long, frustrating history is why the 1990–91 campaign was so special for long-suffering Penguins fans as they watched their beloved team capture a division title, then go on to win three playoff series (after winning only four combined in their entire history), and reach the Stanley Cup Finals for the first time. It had truly been a breakout campaign for the franchise.

As Pittsburgh battled back from a two-games-to-one deficit to Minnesota in the Stanley Cup Finals to win Games Four and Five, the Penguins suddenly found themselves one victory away from achieving the ultimate goal for an NHL team. With another win at the Met Center in Minneapolis, a dream that only a couple years ago seemed unimaginable would finally come true.

Neither the North Stars nor their fans saw Game Six simply as a coronation. A sellout crowd packed into the Met Center anticipating a Minnesota victory that would keep the North Stars' dreams of a title alive. The home team came out aggressive, crashing the Pittsburgh net and launching a shot on goal in the opening seconds. But this aggressiveness only served to fire up the Pens. Before the game was two minutes old, Pittsburgh opened up the scoring when defenseman Ulf Samuelsson lifted what seemed like an innocent shot toward North Star netminder Jon Casey. But Casey was screened and couldn't see the slow shot, which floated past him to give the Penguins a 1–0 lead.

Ten minutes later, Minnesota was on the power play trying to tie the contest. Penguins defenseman Larry Murphy was looking to clear the puck out of his own zone when he sent the puck off the boards and onto the stick of Lemieux, who was gliding into the Stars' zone unabated toward Casey. Lemieux lured Casey away from the net and pulled the puck around him, sliding a backhanded shot into the empty cage for a two-goal advantage.

What chance Minnesota had to continue its Cinderella season was starting to disappear, especially after Pittsburgh went on the power play soon after Lemieux's goal. A shot by Pittsburgh's Joe Mullen was stopped by Casey, but the rebound caromed to Kevin Stevens, who slapped the puck back to Mullen. Mullen then put a quick shot past Casey, who wasn't able to slide over in time. It was 3–0 as the first period ended, and the Penguins were just getting started.

In the past two Penguin victories, Pittsburgh had surged to an early lead only to see the North Stars storm back and turn the contest into a close game, but this time, with the Stanley Cup within their grasp, the Pens would not let up.

Midway through the second period, Pittsburgh made it 4–0 when Bob Errey deflected a shot by Jagr into the net. Two minutes later Mullen stole the puck at center ice and fed it to Ron Francis, who pushed it past backup goalie Brian Hayward, the replacement for the struggling Casey. The onslaught continued as Samuelsson sent a pass right outside his own blue line to Stevens, who tossed a backhanded pass to Mullen at center ice. With the Stars pressing to get on the scoreboard, Mullen was all alone on yet another Pens breakaway. He slipped a shot over Hayward's glove to make it 6–0 going into the third period.

With the game essentially in hand, the Penguins simply needed to run out the final 20 minutes. The break between the second and third periods gave Pittsburgh fans a chance to reflect on all the disappointing times in the past that were about to be overshadowed by what these Penguins were about to accomplish.

The rout continued in the final period. A little over a minute in, Lemieux and defenseman Jim Paek—the first player of Korean descent to play in the NHL—came in on a two-on-one break with Paek sliding the puck around a prone Hayward to give Pittsburgh a seven-goal lead. The Pens rounded out the scoring with just under seven minutes left when Lemieux found Murphy in front of the goal and Murphy flipped a backhanded shot over Casey, who'd reentered the game.

Finally, after 60 long minutes for Minnesota—and 24 long seasons for Pittsburgh—the game came to an end. Mario Lemieux hoisted the Stanley Cup and paraded around the ice as the Penguin nation looked on at a sight they'd never believed possible.

After nearly a quarter century, their ultimate dream had finally come true.

BOX SCORE

Teams	1	2	3	F
Pittsburgh	3	3	2	8
Minnesota	0	0	0	0

Per	Team	Goal (Assist)	Time
1	Pittsburgh	Samuelsson 3 (Taglianetti, Trottier)	2:08
1	Pittsburgh	Lemieux 16 (Murphy)	12:19
1	Pittsburgh	Mullen 7 (Stevens, Taglianetti)	13:16
2	Pittsburgh	Errey 5 (Jagr, Lemieux)	13:15
2	Pittsburgh	Francis 7 (Mullen)	14:28
2	Pittsburgh	Mullen 8 (Stevens, Samuelsson)	18:44
3	Pittsburgh	Paek 1 (Lemieux)	1:19
3	Pittsburgh	Murphy 5 (Lemieux)	13:45

Team	Goalie	Saves	Goals
Pittsburgh	Barrasso	39	0
Minnesota	Casey	13	4
Minnesota	Hayward	7	4

Shots	1	2	3	T
Pittsburgh	11	9	8	28
Minnesota	16	7	16	39

PENGUINS 2, DETROIT RED WINGS 1
JUNE 12, 2009

Max

The annals of Pittsburgh sports history are filled with the heroic tales of a handful of postseason heroes. The Pirates' Bill Mazeroski hit perhaps the most dramatic home run in baseball history to beat the powerful New York Yankees in the 1960 World Series. Roberto Clemente and Willie Stargell both hit clutch long balls to secure Game Seven victories in the Fall Classic in 1971 and 1979. The Steelers' Franco Harris snagged the famed "Immaculate Reception" in the 1972 playoffs, while Santonio Holmes, the former first-round draft pick, made arguably the best catch in Super Bowl history to win Super Bowl XLIII.

It's often said that great players come to the forefront when their teams need them most. For the Pittsburgh Penguins, their Stanley Cup championship run of 2009 had an arsenal of great performers, including Sidney Crosby, Evgeni Malkin, and Marc-Andre Fleury. Each of those players certainly had a hand in guiding the team to Game Seven of the Stanley Cup Finals. Fans hoped one of them would take the team on his back and lift the Penguins to the franchise's third Stanley Cup title.

Ironically, it was a light-scoring French-Canadian center from LeMoyne, Quebec, who etched his name in Steel City lore that evening, as Max Talbot played the game of his life against the heavily favored, defending-champion Detroit Red Wings.

While not a superstar, Talbot did have a track record of performing well in clutch situations. In 2003 and 2004 he led his junior team in the Quebec Major Junior Hockey League to championships while being named the winner of the Guy Lafleur Trophy both seasons as playoff MVP. He scored a last-minute goal in Game Five of the 2008 Stanley Cup Finals with the Pens facing elimination to give Pittsburgh an exciting triple-overtime victory over Detroit. In the 2009 playoffs, he'd inspired his team to victory after it had fallen behind the Flyers in Game Six of their first-round series by picking a fight with the bigger Daniel Carcillo, but all of those moments would be eclipsed as he put on a magnificent offensive performance with the Stanley Cup on the line.

The first two games of the 2009 Stanley Cup Finals had looked very similar to the year before, when Detroit took a two-games-to-none lead with the Red Wings' defense completely stifling the high-powered Pittsburgh offense. The Pens had battled back in 2008 but still lost the series in six games to Detroit. When the Wings also won the first two games in 2009, it appeared as though the Penguins would once again fall to the defending champs.

The fears subsided temporarily when they beat Detroit twice in the Mellon Arena, both by identical 4–2 scores, but after getting crushed 5–0 at the Joe Louis Arena in Game Five, it seemed like only a matter of time before the Wings would hoist the cup for the fifth time in the last 12 seasons. Detroit's Marian Hossa was thrilled at that point as he looked like he had made a wise choice joining the Wings in the off-season in hopes of finally lifting the cup. The former Penguin had turned down Pittsburgh's multiyear offer before the season to sign a one-year contract with Detroit, explaining he felt the Red Wings had a better chance of winning the title than Pittsburgh did.

Unfortunately for Hossa, Pittsburgh held on for a 2–1 victory in Game Six to stay alive, but they would have to return to the Motor City for the seventh and deciding game—in an arena where they'd lost all three times they'd played there in the series. The Penguins also had some history to overcome. No North American major professional sports team had won a seventh game on the road in a championship series in 30 years. Perhaps symbolically, the last to do it was the 1979 Pittsburgh Pirates in the World Series.

Though still underdogs, the Penguins continued the gritty defensive effort they'd displayed the previous contest as they outshot the Red Wings 10–6 in an exciting but scoreless first period.

Early in the second period Talbot began his special evening by pressuring Detroit defenseman Brad Stuart behind the Red Wings' net. Stuart skated toward an aggressive Malkin, who forced the defenseman to make a poor pass, which found its way onto Talbot's stick. Talbot skated in front of Wings netminder Chris Osgood and slid the puck between his legs for a 1–0 Pittsburgh lead.

Just when it appeared the Penguins had momentum, their championship hopes took a blow when Crosby was injured five minutes into the second period. The superstar went into the locker room limping after twisting his leg following a check. While Crosby returned to the bench in the third, he played only one more shift.

With the team's leader essentially out for the rest of the game, Talbot continued to add to his legend. He picked up a loose puck outside his own defensive zone to set up a two-on-one break and put a perfect wrist shot above Osgood's glove to push the Pens' advantage to 2–0.

Twenty minutes away from a championship, Pittsburgh head coach Dan Bylsma decided to turn the game over to his defense and his goaltender to bring home the win. Pittsburgh took only one shot in the final period but limited Detroit to just seven, but three of them threatened to ruin the Penguins' title hopes.

The first scoring opportunity came with only six minutes left in regulation when Detroit defenseman Jonathan Ericsson ripped a slap shot from the point over Fleury's glove and into the net to make it 2–1. Now within a goal of the Pens, the Red Wings continued to pressure Pittsburgh. They came close to tying the contest with 2:14 remaining when Kronwall hit the post with a shot. The Wings had seven-time Norris Award trophy winner Niklas Lidstrom, who was determined to make sure the Pens didn't break that streak.

The Wings had one more chance when they won a face-off in the Pittsburgh zone with only five seconds left. In that tight time frame, the Wings still managed to get a good shot by Niklas Lidstrom, but the shot was blocked by Pens defenseman Hal Gill, and the rebound went back to Lidstrom, who had skated into open ice with 1.5 seconds on the clock. He flicked the puck toward the goal, but Fleury made the save of a lifetime. "I knew there wasn't much time left," Fleury said later. "The rebound was wide. I just decided to get my body out there, and it hit me in the ribs so it was good."[1]

As the puck bounced off Fleury's ribs, the horn sounded, ending the game, the series, and the season. The Penguins mauled their goaltender and then began the celebratory parade with each player skating around the ice with the Stanley Cup joyously over his head. Ironically, one player who could only watch was Hossa. He had been held scoreless in the series and was understandably disappointed with the end result. "Sometimes you make choices," he said. "I still had a great year in this organization. If you score one more, you can celebrate, but if not, they're celebrating. That's life. You just have to move on."[2]

The disappointment the Penguins had experienced when they were turned down by Hossa was forgotten as the celebration continued that night. To the surprise of many, it turned out that they didn't need him after all. They had an unsung hero named Max Talbot on hand to pick up the slack and lead the Penguins to their third Stanley Cup title.

BOX SCORE

Team	1	2	3	F
Pittsburgh	0	2	0	2
Detroit	0	0	1	1

Per	Team	Goal (Assist)	Time
2	Pittsburgh	Talbot 7 (Malkin)	1:13
2	Pittsburgh	Talbot 8 (Kunitz, Scuderi)	10:07
3	Detroit	Ericsson 4 (Lidstrom, Hudler)	13:53

Team	Goalie	Saves	Goals
Pittsburgh	Fleury	23	1
Detroit	Osgood	16	2

Shots	1	2	3	T
Pittsburgh	10	7	1	18
Detroit	6	11	7	24

Notes

#50

1. Associated Press, "Pens Fire Coach Mike Johnston After Sluggish Start," ESPN.com, Dec. 13, 2015, http://espn.go.com/nhl/story/_/id/14348519/pittsburgh-penguins-fire-head-coach-mike-johnston-sluggish-start.

2. Paul Zeise, "Firing Johnston Is Ritheford's Best Move as GM," Pittsburgh Post-Gazette.com, May, 11, 2016, http://www.post-gazette.com/sports/zeise-is-right/2016/05/11/Paul-Zeise-Jim-Rutherford-s-coaching-change-firing-Mike-Johnston-hiring-Mike-Sullivan-Penguins-Stanley-Cup/stories/201605110181.

#49

1. Bob Smizik, "Recchi's Game Returns to Old Form after He Sharpens His Skating," *Pittsburgh Press*, May 24, 1991.

2. Dave Molinari and Bill Modoono, "Murphy Big Plus on Offense and Defense," *Pittsburgh Press*, May 24, 1991.

3. Bill Modoono, "Hayward Makes Most of Bad Times," *Pittsburgh Press*, May 24, 1991.

#48

1. "Sidney Crosby Injured but Penguins Cap Perfect Month of March," ESPN.com, last modified Mar. 30, 2013, http://scores.espn.go.com/nhl/recap?gameId=400442981.

2. Ibid.

#47

1. Bob Barrickman, "Another Look: 'Badger' Bob Johnson," last modified May 10, 2011, www.timesonline.com/sports/another_look/another-look-badger-bob-johnson/article_085d67b2-3ae4-5375-9a1c-04a37073bd26.html.

2. Tom McMillan, "A Great Day for Hockey," *Pittsburgh Post-Gazette*, Nov. 28, 1991.

#45

1. Bob Whitley, "Penguins Sting St. Louis, 5–3," *Pittsburgh Post-Gazette*, Apr. 11, 1975.

#44

1. Dave Molinari, "Lemieux Gets 8 Points in 9–2 Victory," *Pittsburgh Press*, Oct. 16, 1988.

2. Ibid.

#42

1. Dave Molinari, "Sudden Life," *Pittsburgh Press,* May 15, 1995.

2. Ibid.

#39

1. Kevin Allen, "How Did Penguins Third Stringer Jeff Zatkoff Excel on Stanley Cup Stage?" USA Today.com, Apr. 15, 2016, http://www.usatoday.com/story/sports/nhl/2016/04/15/jeff-zatkoff-penguins-goalie-marc-andre-fleury-rangers-stanley-cup-playoffs/83096270/.

2. Ibid.

3. Associated Press, "Patric Hornqvist lifts Penguins Past Rangers with Hat Trick in Opener," ESPN.com, Apr. 14, 2016, http://espn.go.com/nhl/recap?gameId=400874105.

#38

1. Joe Lapointe, "Penguins Glide into the Finals," *New York Times,* May 24, 1992.

2. Associated Press, "Lemieux Fuels Penguins Sweep," *Los Angeles Times,* May 24, 1992.

3. Lapointe, "Penguins Glide into the Finals."

#34

1. Associated Press, "Crosby Elevates Game to Lift Pens as Caps Disappear in Lopsided Game 7," ESPN.com, last modified May 13, 2009, http://sports.espn.go.com/nhl/recap?gameId=290513023.

2. Ibid.

#32

1. Associated Press, "Penguins Finish Off Sweep, in Back-to-Back Stanley Cup Finals," ESPN.com, last modified May 26, 2009, http://sports.espn.go.com/nhl/recap?gameId=290526007.

2. Ibid.

#31

1. "Civic Arena (Pittsburgh)," Wikipedia.com, last modified Dec. 1, 2014.

2. Associated Press, "Penguins Stomp Islanders in Final Regular-Season Game at Mellon Arena," ESPN.com, last modified Apr. 8, 2010, http://sports.espn.go.com/nhl/recap?gameId=300408016.

#30

1. "The Shhhh of Death," NHLPens.com, Apr. 29, 2009.

#29

1. "Mario Lemieux," Penn State library, accessed Dec. 10, 2014, http://pabook.libraries.psu.edu/palitmap/bios/Lemieux__Mario.html.

2. Dave Molinari, "Penguins Take Consolation in Lemieux's Debut," *Pittsburgh Press,* Oct. 12, 1984.

3. Ibid.

#28

1. Tom McMillan, "Pens Win Division," *Pittsburgh Post-Gazette,* Mar. 28, 1991.

#27

1. Dave Molinari, "Devils Provide Scare, but Pens Prevail 4–3," *Pittsburgh Post-Gazette,* Apr. 23, 1993.

#25

1. Associated Press, "Pens Dump Flyers in Game 5 to Reach First Stanley Cup Finals Since '92," ESPN. com, last modified May 18, 2008, http://sports.espn.go.com/nhl/recap?gameId=280518016.

2. Ibid.

#24

1. Associated Press, "Sykora Upends Wings in Third Overtime to Extend Cup Finals," ESPN.com, last modified June 2, 2008, http://sports.espn.go.com/nhl/recap?gameId=280602005.

2. Ibid.

#23

1. Associated Press, "Crosby Scores Shootout Winner as Penguins Nip Sabres in Winter Classic," ESPN.com, Jan. 2, 2008, www.espn.co.uk/nhl/recap?gameId=280101002.

#22

1. Ticker, Game story, USAToday. com, Dec. 27, 2000, http://usatoday30.usatoday.com/sports/scores100/100362/100362332.htm.

#21

1. Jimmy Jordan, "Pens Whip Seals 3–2, Win Series," *Pittsburgh Press,* Apr. 13, 1970.

#19

1. Richard Chere, "Jaromir Jagr: 1999 Goal vs. Devils May Have Saved Pittsburgh Franchise," NJ.com, May 6, 2012, www.nj.com/devils/index. ssf/2012/05/jaromir_jagr_1999_goal_vs_devi.html.

#18

1. Dave Molinari, "Lemieux Gets 5 Goals as Pens Set Record," *Pittsburgh Press,* Apr. 10, 1993.

2. Ibid.

#17

1. Ron Cook, "Pens Give Stars Cause for Pause in Plans," *Pittsburgh Post-Gazette,* May 22, 1991.

2. Ibid.

#16

1. Associated Press, "Conor Sheary's OT Goal Gives Penguins 2–0 Lead over Sharks in Cup Final," ESPN.com, June 2, 2016, http://espn.go.com/nhl/recap?gameId=400877455.

#15

1. Seth Rorabaugh, "Speech Impediment Does Not Slow Down Penguins RW Bryan Rust," Pittsburgh Post-Gazette.com, Jan. 20, 2016, www.post-gazette.com/sports/penguins/2016/01/20/Despite-speech-impediment-Penguins-Bryan-Rust-isn-t-short-on-confidence/stories/201601200036.

#14

1. Tom McMillan, "The Pens End Spectrum Spell," *Pittsburgh Post-Gazette,* Feb. 3, 1989.

2. Ibid.

#13

1. Tom McMillan, "Penguins Advance," *Pittsburgh Post-Gazette,* May 2, 1992.

2. Ibid.

#12

1. Tom McMillan, "Penguins Deck Flyers 10–7," *Pittsburgh Post-Gazette,* Apr. 26, 1989.

#11

1. John S. Chester Jr., interview, "Mike Lange: A National Hockey League Broadcasting Icon," Mar. 7, 2008.

2. Bob Black, "Pens Erase Sabres in Overtime, 4–3," *Pittsburgh Press,* Apr. 15, 1979.

#10

1. Ticker, "Game Story," last modified May 11, 2001, http://sportsillustrated. cnn.com/hockey/nhl/recaps/2001/05/10/ buf_pitt.

2. Ibid.

#9

1. Justin Halbersma, "Interview: Frank Pietrangelo," accessed Dec. 12, 2014, www.openingfaceoff.net/frank-pietrangelo.html.

2. Joe Pelletier, "Frank Pietrangelo," Greatest Hockey Legends (blog), accessed June 13, 2008, http://penguinslegends. blogspot.com/2008/06/frank-pietrangelo. html.

3. Mike Prisuta, "Pens Keep Summer Waiting for Another Night," *Beaver County Times,* Apr. 14, 1991.

#8

1. Filip Bondy, "With Adam Graves' Jersey in Rafters, It's Time to Retire 1994 Ceremonies," *New York Daily News,* Feb. 4, 2009.

2. Bill Utterback, "Penguins Stress Tests Floor Rangers," *Pittsburgh Press,* May 10, 1992.

#7

1. Associated Press, "Penguins Steal Chicago's Game," *Ellensburg Daily Record,* May 27, 1992.

#5

1. "Blackhawks Can't Defy Odds or Deny Penguins," *Milwaukee Journal,* June 2, 1992.

2. "Stanley Cup Finals—Game 4," YouTube, uploaded Mar. 2, 2011, www. youtube.com/watch?v=gm5hpLOw-w0.

3. "Blackhawks Can't Defy Odds," *Milwaukee Journal.*

#4

1. "Pittsburgh Penguins Television and Radio History," Millersville University of Pennsylvania, accessed Dec. 12, 2014, www.millersville.edu/~digitalw/ pa_media_museum/programming/ dwhowe1/myproject.htm.

#1

1. Associated Press, "Fleury Robs Wings in Final Seconds to Secure Stanley Cup for Underdog Penguins," ESPN.com, last modified June 12, 2009, http://sports.espn.go.com/nhl/ recap?gameId=290612005.

2. Ibid.

One for the Ages

When Penguins coach Mike Sullivan took the stage at the parade following the team's Stanley Cup championship in 2016, he mentioned the possibility of meeting there again for a celebration a year later. It was a bold statement; after all, since the National Hockey League instituted the salary cap in 2005, no team had ever successfully defended its title. In fact, it had been 19 years since the Detroit Red Wings had such an achievement, winning the championship in 1997 and 1998. Before the salary cap was instituted, it was a feat reserved for the greats of the game; after the salary cap, it was considered one that was next to impossible, but it was something this group was determined to achieve.

Despite the fact they suffered through an incredible run of injuries that saw their players miss a total of 286 games over the course of the season, including star defenseman Kris Letang, who was gone for the remainder of the campaign with a herniated disk in his neck that required surgery, the team used the formula from the year before: plug the holes with young players from their farm club in Wilkes-Barre and develop a next-man-up philosophy. Players like Carter Rowney, Josh Archibald, Chad Ruhwedel, and Jake Guentzel, a 22-year-old rookie from Omaha, would not only fill in admirably in the regular season but play key roles once the postseason rolled around.

On top of the injuries there was something else that was at the forefront for this team: whether Marc-Andre Fleury would stay in Pittsburgh. Sullivan had decided that rookie Matt Murray was his starter after leading them to the cup the year before, and with the expansion draft coming up—a draft where a team could only protect one goalie—rumors were out there that the Pens' legendary netminder would be traded because the limited no-trade clause that Fleury had in his contract would cause the team to have to protect him. Unbeknownst to all, general manager Jim Rutherford wanted both goalies for the playoff run and made an agreement with Fleury that he would waive any objections about being eligible for the draft so that he could remain with Pittsburgh for the rest

In 13 seasons, Marc-Andre Fleury has become the greatest goaltender in franchise history, winning a team record 375 games, the fifteenth highest total in NHL history. His
tenure in Pittsburgh has come to an end, but he certainly saved his best for last, helping
beat Columbus and Washington in the first two rounds of the 2017 playoffs after substi-
tuting for an injured Matt Murray. (Author's collection)

of the season. It was a decision that would prove fortuitous as Murray tore his
hamstring while warming up for the team's first-round opener against Columbus.

After rolling up an NHL second-best 111 points during the season, in the
first round the team had the unfortunate task—because of the league's bizarre
seeding system—of having to face the fourth-best team in the circuit, the
Columbus Blue Jackets. With their young star goaltender not available for an
extended time, veteran Fleury was given the start. The odds against them not
only repeating, but being able to get out of the first round without Murray and
Letang were long indeed. Luckily for the team, the veteran goalie would be at
the top of his game. Fleury stopped 70 of 72 shots as Pittsburgh swept both
home games to begin the series. After Guentzel notched his first postseason
hat trick in overtime of Game Three, burying a pass from Sidney Crosby, who
led the league in goals during the regular season with 44, to give Pittsburgh a
commanding three-games-to-none lead, the Pens would close out the series
two contests later, winning easier than anyone expected.

Two of the most important players in the back-to-back Stanley Cup championships the Penguins have won are goaltender Matt Murray (*left*) and Nick Bonino (*right*). Murray has won two titles while just completing his official rookie season in 2016–17, winning 22 postseason games during the time period. Bonino has been an integral player for Pittsburgh, scoring eight times in both playoff runs, most of which were memorable. (Author's collection)

The league's strange seeding system again caused Pittsburgh issues in the second round as they faced the team with the best record, the Washington Capitals. After acquiring one of the best defensemen in the league from St. Louis, Kevin Shattenkirk, the experts felt that Washington had done enough to move past Pittsburgh and win their long-awaited first Stanley Cup title. Even though Pittsburgh had defeated Washington in eight of the nine series that the two played in their postseason history, things looked different this time as Washington seemed to be more physical than Pittsburgh, outshooting them 71–45 in the first two games on home ice. The problem was they scored only four times against Fleury while the Pens tallied nine, taking a shocking two-game lead in the series on the road. A cross-check to the head of Crosby by former Penguin Matt Niskanen in Game Three sent the Penguins superstar out of the game with a concussion as the Caps won the contest 3–2 in overtime. Pittsburgh somehow won a close game without their captain in Game Four, but Washington dominated the next two contests, setting up a seventh and

A former Nashville Predator, Patric Hornqvist has been an important part of the Penguins since coming over in the James Neal trade. Hornqvist scored 66 goals in his three seasons in Pittsburgh but none as important as his game winner that gave Pittsburgh its fifth Stanley Cup title against Nashville in Game Six of the 2017 finals. (Courtesy of Cara Finoli)

deciding game in the nation's capital. Unfortunately for the home team, they could not get a puck past Pittsburgh's veteran goalie as Bryan Rust and Patric Hornqvist both scored in a dramatic 2–0 win.

While theoretically it should have gotten easier after dispatching the league's number one and four teams, the Ottawa Senators were playing well and were a formidable opponent. The Pens offense was sluggish in the first three games as the physical Senators defense limited them to three goals as Ottawa won two, including a one-sided 5–1 victory in Game Three that saw Sullivan replace Fleury with a now healthy Murray. Murray played magnificently as Pittsburgh won the next two contests, including a dominant 7–0 Game Five victory. After losing Game Six 2–1, the teams returned to the Steel City for a Game Seven that was one for the ages. The teams were tied at two at the end of regulation and went into a second overtime before Chris Kunitz scored one of the greatest goals in team history, giving the Pens a 3–2 to win and a spot in the finals against the upstart Nashville Predators.

It seemed like Pittsburgh was playing against more than a hockey team; they were playing against a rabid fan base that was insistent on throwing catfish on the ice, even at the PPG Paints Arena and at the entire country music nation. For four games Nashville seemingly got the better of the play, including holding the Penguins shotless for 37 minutes in Game One, although somehow Pittsburgh won 5–3 on a late Guentzel goal, one of a league-leading thirteen he scored in the postseason, the second-highest rookie total in Stanley Cup playoff history. They also won Game Two 4–1 before the Predators dominated the defending champions at home in the next two contests, tying the series at two as they returned to Pittsburgh for Game Five. After scoring 13 times against Murray in four games, the Predators would score no more. Pittsburgh played its best game of the postseason, not only winning 6–0 but beating them physically as Crosby was magnificent.

In Game Six at Nashville, the teams played an even, exciting contest when the Predators appeared to break the scoreless tie midway in the second period. Colton Sissons dove in toward a rebound, tipping it in to give Nashville a 1–0 lead. Unfortunately, the referee lost sight of the puck and blew the whistle before Sissons scored, negating the goal. The game continued to be scoreless as the Pens fought off several penalties, including a five-on-three disadvantage midway in the third. Finally, with only 1:35 remaining in regulation, Hornqvist tipped the puck off goalie Pekka Rinne to give Pittsburgh a 1–0 lead. The Pens defense stifled Nashville the rest of the way as Carl Hagelin ended the contest with 14 seconds left, netting an empty net goal that clinched the Penguins' fifth Stanley Cup championship.

Despite the myriad of injuries that continued to plague the team during the postseason—which included Murray's torn hamstring, Nick Bonino's broken ankle, Crosby's concussion, Hagelin's broken fibula, Brian Dumolin's injured hand, Hornqvist's broken fingers, and Justin Schultz's cracked ribs—the next-man-up philosophy endured as the team did something no one gave them a chance to do: become the first salary cap–era back-to-back Stanley Cup champions.

Top Penguins Games in the 2017 Stanley Cup Playoffs

5. GAME 5: Stanley Cup Finals. Pittsburgh 6, Nashville 0.
4. GAME 4: Eastern Conference second round.
   Pittsburgh 3, Washington 2.
3. GAME 7: Eastern Conference second round.
   Pittsburgh 2, Washington 0.
2. GAME 7: Eastern Conference Finals. Pittsburgh 3, Ottawa 2.
1. GAME 6: Stanley Cup Finals. Pittsburgh 2, Nashville 0.